Poetry Ireland Review 120

Eagarthóir / Editor
VONA GROARKE

© Poetry Ireland Ltd 2016

Poetry Ireland Ltd/Éigse Éireann Teo gratefully acknowledges the assistance of The Arts Council/An Chomhairle Ealaíon and The Arts Council of Northern Ireland.

Poetry Ireland invites individuals and commercial organizations to become Friends of Poetry Ireland. For more details, please contact:

Poetry Ireland Friends Scheme, Poetry Ireland, 11 Parnell Square East, Dublin 1, Ireland

or telephone +353 1 6789815; e-mail info@poetryireland.ie

FRIENDS:
Joan and Joe McBreen, Desmond Windle, Neville Keery,
Noel and Anne Monahan, Ruth Webster, Maurice Earls,
Mary Shine Thompson, Seán Coyle, Henry and Deirdre Comerford,
Thomas Dillon Redshaw, Rachel Joynt

ISBN: 1-902121-63-5
ISSN: 0332-2998

ASSISTANT EDITORS: Paul Lenehan, Daniel Tatlow-Devally, and Sally Rooney

IRISH-LANGUAGE EDITOR: Liam Carson

DESIGN: Alistair Keady (www.hexhibit.com)

COVER CREDIT: from 'Dr. Nadia Kelbova', photograph by Justyna Kielbowicz
http://justynakielbowicz.com

Contents

Editorial

The Rising Generation questionnaire from *Poetry Ireland Review* 118

Were you a strange child with a taste for verse? I still am.

Do you too dislike it? Not the idea of it. Not the best of it. Not the impulse. But let's face it, most of what calls itself poetry is god-awful. Writing a good poem is *hard* and it's hardly ever accomplished. It's important to dislike the mediocre, self-important, cheaply-made, insincere or spineless poem, because only then can there be imaginative allowance for the extraordinary one.

Who is your favourite character in a poem? The speaker of Philip Larkin's 'Going'. There's courage for you; courage to see, to feel, to be fearful, and still to ask a hard question, and to ask it elegantly.

If you could die and come back as a poem, what poem would it be? John Donne's 'The Sun Rising'. 'Busy old fool, unruly sun': oh, all that glamour and ploy.

Someone offers you €1,000,000 to never write again: What is your response? I'm Irish: haven't you ever heard of the 'empty formula'?

Have you ever glued pages of a poetry book together? God, yeah. Tight as my lips are now.

It's the centenary of the Easter Rising: does this fact matter to you and if so, in what way? Less and less. (It's December, after all).

If someone described you as a political poet, what would your reaction be? That depends. If it were a politician, for example, I'd aim for the head when I threw my ballot box. And yet. I have just written a book about being, as much as anything, a middle-aged woman: I defy anyone to say that's not a political gesture. And yet. I tend to run from the word 'politics'. I'm for words with a bit more truth and energy packed in. But words, I know, are political tools, and they don't shuck that off because they choose to hide out in a poem for a while. Let's say, then, that I'm not a political poet, but even a poet with her back to politics will still face the way it does.

Would you rather be the poet or the poem? The poem, of course, silly. The poet may stand behind the poem, but the successful poem won't care. It needs nothing, least of all my continued fumblings and mutterings. Wouldn't that be an ideal state, to need nothing anymore?

If you could pick a time to be dropped amongst the three best poets alive at that moment, when would it be and who would they be? Now. When poetry isn't sequestered into privileged corrals. (Or at least, not always and necessarily). Now. When so much good work has already been made, and it seems a tall order to be fresh and stylish and crafty and wise, and to admit you have to be. The stakes are high. But look, there's the Carson Family, Anne and Ciaran, striding out to the microphones. And Louise Glück and Alice Oswald are tuning up a storm to raise the dead. Here comes every-one! What a gig! And I can't see the half of it. Surprise me, do.

What's your worst poetry habit? The word 'that'.

You've arranged a date for 8pm, but it's 8.10pm now. You're working on a poem and it's going well. What do you do? Hold on a minute, the poem's 'going well'? But doesn't every self-respecting poem go badly, until it doesn't go anymore? Badness is more interesting. Now I've created a problem, and I can't just get up and leave without solving it, or trying to. So, I'm going to stick with the poem. He'll know where to find me, if he wants. But that poem will slip through my hands like rain, if I don't see it through.

Have you ever carried a poem by someone else around on your person? If so, what was it? I've carried books in my bag, and lines in my head; rarely whole poems, not even my own. I've learned not to over-estimate headspace capacity.

A family member says, 'You should write a poem about that.' What do you do? I like to think I pull a wet herring from a specially sealed bag kept for such occasions, and use it to slap the person's cheek while explaining that poems are not anecdotes and that probably the least important aspect of any good poem is what it is *about*. But of course, I don't. I smile and play dead, imagining a very quiet room in which I forage for myself, and no one serves me subject matter, on a swish or a bockety tray.

If your best poem were a weekend away, where would it be? A B&B in Bally-mahon. In February. In flagrant rain.

It's a good poem but it's forty-one lines long and the competition with the big prize specifies a max of forty: what do you do? Hang the prize. The poem's the thing, and it imagines its own rules.

Have you ever used a poem to seduce someone? If so, what poem was it? (And did it work?). I'll plead the fifth dimension on this one (as a man once did in a US court. And then he disappeared).

You're given a choice: either every poem or no poem you write from now on must use the word 'I'. Which do you choose? Every poem. 'I' is probably the most dangerous and dynamic word at a poet's disposal. Introduce it into a poem and the game changes instantly. But I can see why people are wary of it, it's such a sly little thing. Two-faced. Half the time, it's not even interested in itself, it's just throwing shapes.

Your friend is depressed: what's the very last poetry book you'd give him / her? 'You Made Me Late Again!' by Pam Ayres. Can you imagine anything worse? All that jollity and metre, plus an exclamation mark!

Who will play the poet in the Hollywood adaptation of your last poem? Kathy Bates. Or Harvey Keitel (if the car insurance ads dry up, he might be available). Or what about Jennifer Lawrence? (The midlands accent might be tricky, but she's a versatile actress – the rest ought to be a cinch).

You're invited to read in a major festival: what are your top three backstage demands? A teabag. A kettle. Quite a lot of milk. (If they can lay on Liam Neeson to make the tea, that would be quite nice. Tell him Jennifer Lawrence will be there. And that she's fond of tea).

What's your current favourite word? Bolthole.

You're proud of the poem but know it will offend someone you don't even like: what do you do? Write it. Resolve to go out less. That should solve the problem.

Would you rather win the TS Eliot Prize or the Prize Bonds? The Prize Bonds. No poem I'd ever write in the future need know a thing about it.

Let's assume you're 60 and still publishing poems: what do you want to have achieved between now and then? 60? Good god, who writes this stuff? (Sigh). Well, then. A collection of poems that is way better than any I've published thus far.

Cyril Connolly said the true function of a writer is to write a masterpiece, and no other task is of any consequence. Do you agree? Yes. If possible. (Of course, the true function of a human being could be a different thing).

'The hard part is getting to the top of page 1' – Tom Stoppard. What, for you, is the hard part? Time. And the finding of it. Not just for writing, but for the gradual levering of oneself into writing, that involves a lot of reading and looking out of windows and not answering e-mails or, heaven forfend, questionnaires. Either that, or the handling of the moment you know the whole thing's gone to hell; when I write and write and I simply can't

get life into any of it; when it's vivid as a bowl of steam. When I am loud as stones in a bucket or when I'm just imitating myself. What an echo-chamber that can be. Getting out of *that*, that's the hard part.

If your ideal poem were an outfit, what would it look like? An indigo, bias-cut, *crêpe de Chine* evening dress with jet beading, fusible interfacing, honey-comb pleats and a running hem. All stitched by notions, of course. Which I'd wear with Converse or possibly, winklepickers. I'd be wearing language. And listening, every movement, to the gorgeous rustle of words.

What advice would you give to older poets? Read younger poets. Resist disap-pointment. Shed opinions and fixed positions. Try at least once to write something different to anything you've written so far.

Is there any question you wish you'd been asked here (that you'd like to answer now)? What on earth were you thinking of, answering this questionnaire?

And is there anything you'd like to add? (Since this is by way of a tooraloora, the editor might just allow some latitude on word count).

Blame Paul Lenehan, the publications manager: this was his idea. 'You know that questionnaire', says he, 'the one for The Rising Generation issue? For a final editorial, why don't you answer it yourself?' And so I have, mindful that an editor should always take the advice of such an excellent publications manager, without whose careful eye and even hand these past eight issues could have turned out a mare's nest.

But I don't think they did. We have published some good poems, which is no mean boast for a poetry magazine. Some smart, alert reviews. And interviews and essays that help to expand an understanding of what's afoot in our poetry.

It's been fun. I read many lively and well-turned-out poems, and others I enjoyed meeting, even if I couldn't publish them. So, thanks to you readers and subscribers; thanks to you poets and reviewers for being game; and thanks to you all at Poetry Ireland – together you made my tenure here an adventure, a good lark.

To incoming editor, Eavan Boland, I send an excited, anticipatory greeting, and a single cautionary note: beware of setting any question-naires, now you see what comes of it.

– Vona Groarke

Ciaran Berry

EXTRA TERRESTRIAL

The flowers die, the flowers come back to life.
Through the rainbow blinds, I point towards my lost star.
It's like I'm that sad usher waving her torch
along the rows of the Astor Cinema to make sure
the courting couples haven't gone too far.
Crushed Coca-Cola cans, Monster Munch,
Sam Spudz Thicker Crinkled Cheese 'n' Onion. The smell
of popcorn and of piss from the men's room.

I throw a ball into the dark, the ball comes back.
I step once more into the backyard of it, light washing
through the slats of the unkempt garden shed.
Its rakes and hoes. Its charcoal and lawn seed.
I sit out in a deck-chair, wait for whatever it is
to take a form. I leave a trail of Skittles or M&Ms
on the off chance it might follow me home –
this creature who is me and not me I'll conceal

behind the bedroom closet's louvered doors,
his head nothing anyone would ever look for
amidst the one-eyed teddy bears and GI Joes.
The way his skin is stretched across his bones
puts me in mind of some ageing relative
whose veins begin to show through the translucence
like the curves and discursions of a back road.
Whin bushes and fuchsia, oak and ash, potholes.

A strip of grass running down the middle
like a Mo-Hick haircut as my aunt was wont to say
of what must be Dolan's Lane or Dolan's Brae.
I take the long way round again so as not to be seen
in my Lord Anthony coat and my bell bottom jeans.
His sacred heart, his telescopic limbs
remind me I'm space cadet, I'm alien,
a blow-in on my way home with messages.

Soup meat wrapped in brown paper. In waxed paper,
a sliced pan. A plastic bag of bones the dog
will bury in the ground where later we'll bury him.
I carry it all in the basket of my mother's Raleigh Shopper
that I wish were a BMX, or a Chopper,
a flame motif across the double crossbar
on which my cousin, acting the goat, will split
his scrotum right between the stones. To think

of it is to cross your legs like that girl in the back row
who fears things are about to go too far,
her souped-up lover staring at the screen,
where those two brothers sniff the warp and weft
of their absent father's shirt for the scent
of Sea Breeze or is it Old Spice, as his hand
climbs the incline of her thigh. I lie down
beside it again, go eye to eye with it. The spilled milk

on the kitchen floor. The cold sweat on a can
of Coors. I finger the dial of that transmitter and receiver
conjured from a circular saw blade, a record player,
the keyboard from a Speak 'n' Spell. I hold
my ear up to the unlabelled baked bean tin of it
and hope you'll pick up at the other end
and talk to me along this piece of string. It's been too long,
and what I want now more than anything

is that moment when the bikes shift skywards
in a sudden swell of strings above the hillside
of the half-built suburban dream. Redwoods and cornfields.
The tinkle of a nearby stream. Everything
balanced on the handlebars and freewheeling,
like a boy kicking his Nikes or Adidas through midair.
The steady skitter of the reel. The tractor beam
of the projector. Before all of this puncture and repair.

Miriam Gamble

THE OAK THAT WAS NOT THERE

The oak that was not there was not there
and the sands went walking under the sea.

The clocks went forward, the clocks went back.
Someone lost their temper with me.

From a hillock, we looked on as water
swept its grey silk garment through the estuary.

The clocks went forward, the clocks went back.
The penitent, down on his knees, begged

for the honey of forgiveness from a round god
whose presence we had proven.

The clocks went forward, the clocks went back;
there was no response. But we must act responsibly!

said our grave leader as the flowers of the machair
grew scissor faces. On their faces,

the hands of the second went chop, chop, chop;
the digitalis ate a mink. To think,

one murmured, That it should come down to this.
Another nodded: I consent there is something wrong –

as the blown-glass nimbi angled and clinked
and the clocks went back and forwards, back and forwards –

Where is the oak, for one thing? Where is the blasted oak?
And the round god fell from the sky like a fish.

Paul Henry

CLIFF TERRACE CLOUDS

The summer's clouds are moving east.
My father stokes their fires.

They do not know it is winter,
that I am already old.

Over the Sugarloaf they go,
full of my mother's songs.

Over the hill's white pebbles,
away, away from the sea.

Rachael Boast

TWO POEMS AFTER AKHMATOVA

Hand, Match, Ashtray

We are sitting here to memorise the poem
before the pages I have wrapped myself in
are taken off, like a pleated dress, and burned
over an ashtray. The matches are there on the table.

This pain is not just our own; we have
a thousand hands; we are a forest of birches
outside the devastated city, tired of ordeals,
and of the tortured metal of icons we remain silent.

I mean to offer you the sound of bells ringing out
from a far away abandoned church, the smell
of scorched rafters and rubble, to say that fire
is also light. All this I saw in the mirror,

and in the dream of the mirror, your figure
hurrying across fields to a room with no walls,
where the body is poem. We held each other
in that room, and, for a moment, there was no pain.

To Akhmatova

Cold sharp syntax of snow lying on the ground
beneath a sky so deeply blue you mistake it
for her eyes. Snow in Odessa where the snow-white
waves rush in off the Black Sea, where water
feeds on the weather. Snow in the parks of Leningrad
where the snow-white statues weep. But it is better
that they weep. In her eyes, the hard mastery of thaw.

Seán Hewitt

TREMORS

Alice Lyons, *The Breadbasket of Europe* (Veer Books, 2016), £15.
Blake Morrison, *Shingle Street* (Chatto and Windus, 2015), £10.
Bernard O'Donoghue, *The Seasons of Cullen Church* (Faber and Faber, 2016), hb £12.99.

In the second section of Alice Lyons' minimal but vast new work, the speaker contemplates the ephemerality of her movements over New York, Ukraine, and Ireland, trying to make sense of her own unpindownable self: 'a person is a subset of decisions / selected from the larger set of all possibilities'. Now, one might also say that the set of possibilities determines the decision, that the power lies with the possibilities rather than the person deciding, but the sometimes frantic, other times serene and wise voice of *The Breadbasket of Europe* reveals an intent to reclaim or at least understand the power of the self in an abstracted world:

> today: yolk-yellow schoolbus
> revolving door of Standard Hotel
> taxicabs
>
> chair I choose

In this long book, divided into a number of sections and packed with typographical illustrations and coloured pages, the 'real' world is minimized, and becomes a sort of flickering background to the flighty speaker.
    Lyons' acute eye for linguistic detail and pagination is equally effective in both her cityscapes and seascapes (there is a remarkable passage about swimming to Inishmurray that is reminiscent of Thomas A Clark), and even in its small syntactical fragments it allows the anxieties and conflicts of the wider world to seep through. The song of a skylark is introduced as a 'relentless Morse-code modem shriek' in the 'ceaseless infostream of Inishmurray'; ominously, 'words are ice floes / melting steadily'. This sense of language and the voice being infiltrated, of words as fractious and vulnerable to pressure, leads to a self-conscious questioning of the place of the lyric in a globalized world where geopolitics threatens to overtake the watertight personal experience of the moment. One poem, 'For people to type language on onionskin …' considers the uneven development of Europe against the foil of post-Tiger Ireland: '*I told you, we'll be back on the potatoes*'. There are moments when the experiments seem to flail (the sections of 'The Whaling Log' have too much forced

comedy, and the voice seems a little uninhabited), and other times when the question of audience (Lyons is an American poet living in Ireland) leads the writer to stop and give awkward explanations mid-poem ('Potato ridges are long curved lines on the green hillsides of Ireland'), but as a total work *Breadbasket* is wide in scope, engaging and fresh. If the pagination and occasional handwritten lines seem a little overworked, the quality of the opening few sections alone show us that Lyons can pull off brave and crystalline poetry.

Blake Morrison's *Shingle Street*, his first full-length collection for nearly thirty years, shows a similar vulnerability to the infiltration of the political. A sequence of nine poems at the heart of the collection, each of which begins with 'This poem ...', deftly explores the implications of war, mass surveillance, celebrity scandals, and hacking on the fabric of poetic form. There are moments when Morrison's poetry teeters on the Larkin-esque, with the best poems in the collection ('Evacuation', 'Cottage Down a Lane', 'Old Men Sighing') offering sharp and poignant glimpses of possible lives. These are meditations on the condition of old age, passed down from our parents and later caught and experienced with unexpected familiarity.

In 'Happiness', one of the most understated and arresting poems in *Shingle Street*, we are given a list of tangible glimpses of joy – 'Toasted granary bread with damson jam, / a pair of goldfinches on the bird-feeder' – which are undercut in the very last phrase: 'Two deckchairs in the shade of a weeping birch. / Everyone you love still alive, last time you heard.' Those final four words, speaking of the insecurity of the pastoral vision which precedes them, resonate with this collection's constant probing at the agents of change, ecological and social crisis, which (as in Morrison's earlier work) seep uncomfortably into his use of traditional, somewhat bouncy metrical and rhyming structures.

In other poems, however, that sense of insecurity, or the desire to make the reader feel the discomfort of the speaker, seems less controlled, and can leave us questioning whether it is the poet or the poem which is making us uncomfortable. In 'Carissimo', for example, two swimmers ('we') arrive on a sandbank (or 'yellow colony'),

> and marched about as if we owned the place,
> two giants on an unmapped island,
> the waves like excited natives
> clamouring round our feet.

Although the final line of the poem, in which the speaker tries to decipher his partner's repeated whisper ('I thought it was "trespassers"'), seems designed to have us side with the poet, the poem's ruse to make us condemn the language by couching it as a mistake, or as an allusion to Swift's Gulliver, seems perhaps a little too difficult to pull off. Likewise, in the poem 'Rape', there is a conflation of the flower and the crime which catches the reader off guard, and toes a very fine line between poetic artifice and genuine discomfort. These examples are by no means typical of this collection, which is generally characterized by clear elegiac poems that showcase an impressive willingness to embrace a variety of forms, but they reveal the instability of poetic voice, which seeps through both *Shingle Street* and Lyons' *Breadbasket*.

Bernard O'Donoghue's *The Seasons of Cullen Church* is the work of a poet at the height of his powers. As with Morrison's collection, *Cullen Church* is predominantly elegiac, its typical mode the past tense lyric. But these poems are understated, honest, quietly brutal; they may look back to the Cork of O'Donoghue's childhood, but they are contemporary in scope and reference. In 'Stigma', there is a sense of guilt inherent in the looking back: the speaker considers a farm worker who was employed on the family farm, detailing over four stanzas a whole life in exact and moving detail, before ending with the question:

> Why not stay
> with the poverties of our present time:
> beggars on bridges for us to trip on,
> or asylum-seekers loping through
> the infra-red at detention centres
> on the coast of France, or drowning
> in their hundreds in the Med?

There is a pull between the core of the poem and its final thought, between the elegiac mode and contemporary concerns, but as ever with O'Donoghue's work, things are not so simple. The life of the farm worker acts as a proxy for these ills: as in Lyons' *Breadbasket*, modern Ireland's history of emigration, poverty and subsistence rears its head in the face of the pressing concerns of global development and the migration crisis, leading the poets to a sensitive questioning of the lyric of rural life.

O'Donoghue has long been rightly celebrated for his translations of Anglo-Saxon and Middle English poetry, and this collection gives us a hint at his forthcoming version of Langland's epic *Piers Plowman* in the form of a touching translation ('The Boat') dedicated to the late Seamus Heaney. Another poem rendered from the Middle English ('The Move') has all of O'Donoghue's understated sensitivity. Here, the poet excavates a short lyric about a lover moving away which becomes a meditation on loneliness and age that resonates with other poems in the collection – 'First Night There' in particular ends with the echo of an emptiness that the poet and poem work to fill:

> But still
> there will be the tremor of the memory
> of the dark evening when you had to people
> the whole empty lifescape on your own.

The sense of the body and the mind having to heal themselves is a key theme in *The Seasons of Cullen Church*. 'Stigmata', one of the most heartrending of the elegies in the collection, takes a single image of a dead man's 'chapped hands / folded across his chest in the city morgue'. The fact that the hands have now lost their capacity to heal is turned to poignant effect, and is rooted again in the hardships of a remembered way of life. In each of these collections, the past confronts the present as a haunting, which in the best poems becomes central to the very act of writing, the infiltration of wider concerns putting pressure on the form. In O'Donoghue's work, with its hint of spirituality and its restraint, the poems bear these tensions effortlessly. In 'Swifts', one of the last poems in the collection, this return is imagined on an island off the coast (perhaps not new territory for Irish writing), but it chimes with the other poems in this global and deeply human work:

> ... the presence of the returning swallows
> that Eoghaneen watched for every spring,
> or the shearwaters who were all around us
> one mystic Skellig midnight, souls returned
> from their other, closed life deep out at sea.

Jacob Polley

DARK SEASONS
  – after Baudelaire

I love the seasons dark, the nights brought down
like blackout cloths and puddles turned to stone.
I love the creaking boards and spiders' webs,
the rat-shot cupboard of my empty head

and crypt of nibbled books I lie inside,
hardly breathing but glad I haven't died
and live to feel the draughts that slam the doors
and hear the weathercock squeal itself hoarse.

No warmth for me, no bursting forth, no spring:
my soul unfurls its bright black raven's wings
when all the trees are hollow-eyed as skulls.

I want nothing to change unless it dulls
to the blinded silver of the winter moon,
staring like a face from a breath-fogged spoon.

Jacob Polley

POEM WITH A TWENTY-THREE-YEAR GAP

He split the elder stick with my penknife,
the white pith like the foam
in a slashed car seat. His life
ran out in the cold, two streets from home.

Sinéad Morrissey

THE SINGING GATES

Up on top of Divis on a freezing Saturday
we pass the singing gates: five five-barred silver yokes

across from the café (closed for renovation),
penning nothing in but their own frustration.

They keen like washerwomen into the billowing sky.
You're talking Batman, Two-Face, Robin; you lope

ahead and circle and run back, ready to walk
for hours if we have time, free at last of school

and all the worksheets you never manage to finish
on your own. I can no longer ask my grandad

exactly how his release was managed back in April
'45: five years of his young man's life wiped out

for being a so-called enemy of the State in wartime
(that other bout of internment no one ever mentions)

and then what? Tipped out onto the pavement like a sack
of damaged apples as the gates of Crumlin Road Gaol

clanged shut behind him? My father says he walked
to this summit the very next morning, walked

to work every day thereafter, walked to think,
walked for pleasure, walked to stretch each inch of his cell

by laying it down, over and over, on the floor
of the borderless world, so that its chipped-tile cast-iron

rectangle could disappear... We opt for the Ridge Trail,
a heathery zigzag that wraps the whole side of the hill

in its ribbon while The Joker secedes to mummification
and the death rites of Ancient Egypt. You're a dark-haired

flurry in a hailstorm, running on sugar and bliss,
who can't tell *b* from *d* because *any* letter might just flick

its Fred Astaire hat and dance backwards across the page
if it felt like it, yet starving all the same for knowledge –

imbibing the French Revolution or species of cacti
like brawn and remembering everything.

My grandad brought his own son here from the age of four
on crippling, all-day hikes on Saturdays

(long before, as the Jesuits saw it, my father had the capacity
for resistance to anything) and told him brilliant stories:

the Battle of Stalingrad, the Defence of the Luding Bridge,
The Great Only Appear Great Because We Are On Our Knees,

Let Us Rise – until the two of them fell asleep
in Hatchet Field, clouds passing over their faces like zeppelins.

The oil rigs you fell in love with
a year ago are still moored at the shipyard's glittering edge.

Storms of gunmetal grey touch down precisely in far-off
tinkertoy villages though for now we're walking in sunshine,

welcome as any downpour after a drought, as you list
the typical contents of a sarcophagus and detail the risk

of double jeopardy in the Hall of Two Truths –
Did you bring joy? Did you find joy? –

Horus skulking hawk-eyed in the background.
For most of my father's childhood, my grandad must have looked

like the man in the black-and-white photograph I keep sequestered
in a notebook: a Guest of Honour in the Soviet Union, turned Italian

in the Black Sea sunshine, his hallmark Donegal suit
dramatically cut, skinny like you and even more electric,

a honey magnet (and he knew it) for secretaries, receptionists,
stray passing female fellow revolutionaries

in that dim hermetic time lock called Transport House
with its tea trolleys, telephone exchanges,

ash trays standing guard along corridors
like Russian Babushkas in apartment blocks.

We can pick out its derelict white-black-and-turquoise
(Belfast's only example of Socialist Realist architecture)

from the rest of the city centre's humdrum colours.
Do you want to ask me a question, Mummy?

(by far your favourite question) as we come up at last
by our circuitous route to the granite triangulation point

where, three months earlier, my grandad's children
and their children and their children took turns with a kitchen scoop

to launch what was left of him into the air.
He'd made himself so small in the previous months,

perhaps out of courtesy, it hadn't been hard
and I want to ask you about the gates

we're on our way back to – what wind caught where?
In what cavity? Why this particular calibre of sound

unravelling only here? Are they in harmony? Are they a choir?
Are they, in fact, the singing ticket to the afterlife

and how might we post ourselves into it, limb by limb?
What scarab? What amulet? What feather? What scale? What spell?

Paul Batchelor

SONG

'Make my bed with all things green;
Love is easy lost and won ...'
Half-forgotten, the refrain
Answers to itself alone.

We who took that tendered phrase
For a sign or wedding vow
Thinking it was meant for us
Cannot look for pardon now.

Should you turn to speak to me –
Love forestalled, hope in your eyes –
What would I feel but dismay,
Mild remorse and mild unease?

Out of silence comes the true
Saying every poet hears,
Self-consoling answer to
All the human heart requires;

Nothing you could call a tune,
Nothing I'd claim as my own:
Make my bed with all things green.
Love is easy lost and won.

Paul Batchelor

THE MATTER

> *as if heaven cared*
>> – John Wieners

After sleepy time, pain. After sin, self-knowledge.
The world is all we waken to. Let mother
lick a hanky, kneel to rub the matter
from our clogged eyes: there. After an age

of small mercies, the predictable travesty.
After a lifetime of supportable losses,
a woman bibbed in gin & vomit rises
to disavow a prodigal & would-be

righteous anger. Let dormative potions take
effect. Let one he knows, but not to speak to,
smile recognisably. Non è fuggito.
Now be a love for heaven's sake

and let it go. Who wants to make a scene?
Her least of all, who would & will affect
to misconceive me at my most direct;
knew I meant well, never knows what I mean.

Michael Symmons Roberts

MY FATHER'S DEATH

I don't believe in omens,
but that wedding bowl in smithereens,
then the starling in our hallway
whose fear sent the dog into a fury,

then those cast-in-blue recurrent dreams
in which he visits me and seems
aware of some unspoken threat
from which I wake in dread, *and yet*,

and yet he is still here, *thank God*. Am I
dry-running for that day,
as if to preview loss might stem its force,
and so he goes, and goes, and goes?

I need to break its hold.
I set a trap, an apple iced with mould,
heavy with its sick perfume:
open window, north-facing room.

I sit in wait and watch it land:
my father's death, close up, new-spawned
or rather, hatched,
so purposeful in dreams, now, watched,

can barely hold its line in air,
I speak out loud an ancient prayer
I only half-believe
and on the s of *save*

it flutters to my hand and look,
its iridescent jet, its wings of black lacework,
the hidden kernel of a rose,
a gothic wind-up toy. I close

my fist on it, too slow, it's gone.
You parasite, you origami con,
you blow-in, mayfly, duff lit spill,
now go, and never come again. I know you will.

Michael Symmons Roberts

THE COLD

Despite this blizzard, or because of it,
the dog wants letting out. In summer she was white,

but now she can't compete. Instead,
she starts to eat it off what was the road,

as if by this brute method she can free us.
Outgunned, outnumbered, she looks up at the geese

in their *greater-than* formation cutting low over
the roofs, and I, at this half-opened door

– dressed for an inner life, facing an outer –
know neither one thing nor the other.

Sky is blank, and endless blank, but that was never
the place to find a cure for this cold fever.

If prayers are heard, as I believe they are,
then they are heard here without fear or favour,

and the answers must be here too, solid and sure.
Across the road, swaddled, my neighbour

the retired accountant scrapes and shovels
out beyond his drive into the street, and still it falls.

I try to reckon up if I should go to him,
if the rate of two digging could win us this game,

or if we should give in to it, wait for the melt.
God of the snows, I know this is my fault,

I have kept your voice too distant, hard to pick out
from the freight trains, cold calls, backchat,

when I should feel your breath against my cheek,
words so clear that I could not mistake

your answers for my own. So here, a prayer
for the frostbitten feet of Captain Oates, whose Terra Nova

ended in a walk off the edge of the earth,
for the hands of Francis Bacon, who met death

while trying to stuff a fowl with ice,
for the deep sounded lungs of Louis MacNeice,

who caught his in a cave recording echoes,
for the kicked-out, street-sleepers, hawkers and strays,

for the eyes of a driver hunched over his wheel,
for the hearts, lungs, lights that make us real,

I stare into the beautiful nil, winter's empyrean,
then scrap that prayer and start again.

Alice Lyons

THE WRITING IS NOT *ABOUT* SOMETHING. THE WRITING *IS* SOME-
THING: THREE TAKES

Kim Moore, *The Art of Falling* (Seren Publishing, 2015), £9.99.
Sarah Howe, *Loop of Jade* (Chatto and Windus, 2015), £10.
Vahni Capildeo, *Measures of Expatriation* (Carcanet Press, 2016), £9.99.

Anne Carson was in Santa Fe last week care of the Lannan Foundation
to read from her new book, *Float*, and was interviewed on stage afterwards by Michael Silverblatt, whose author-interview show *Bookworm*
(on KCRW in LA, available as a podcast on their site) is an oasis in the
sorry desert of the US airwaves. Silverblatt had interviewed Anne Carson
on enough previous occasions to be prepared for curtness on good days
and, on bad days, a Dylan-esque impetuousness, which is annoying.
(If you don't want to be interviewed, don't do interviews, right?). But
Silverblatt disarmed the poet with informed enthusiasm and love, which
she warmed to. In fact, he drew her out more than I've ever seen her be
drawn out with a question about her style, which he called 'tight-lipped'.
She agreed. Said it ran deep in her family, from her banker father who
uttered two words to her on the way to her wedding, to a deaf uncle who
lived as a hermit in the Canadian woods and who supposedly only uttered
five or six sentences in his life. Then Silverblatt said, 'The writing is not
ABOUT something. The writing IS something', and I watched people in
seats around me scribble this down in their Moleskines.
    Which I did, too, though I wrote it next to the handsome photo of
Carson in the Lannan reading series program, printed on lavishly heavy
card stock that I'd been handed when I took my seat. The ABOUT versus
IS writing continuum seemed a fitting lens with which to look at these
three books, all of which succeed in various ways with writing that most
assuredly IS something but could easily be oversimplified by an emphasis
on the more superficially and readily-grasped ABOUT qualities of each.
    You could say there is a lot of ABOUT in Kim Moore's debut collection
The Art of Falling. 'My People', the book's second poem, locates Moore
among the white working classes of the North of England, 'people who
swear without realising they're swearing' ; 'scaffolders and plasterers
and shoemakers and carers'. As the publisher's notes on the book jacket
describe, the poet 'sets out her stall firmly in the North', which could be
dangerously quaint and superficial (the colourful people and language of
the North!). But Moore brings an unflinching eye that rescues the book
from essentialising her community and herself as a member of it. The
best poems in *The Art of Falling* see Moore both implicating her speakers

in *and* extricating themselves from their origins. The poem 'Tuesday at Wetherspoons' is indicative of the delicate balance Moore manages throughout the book. The poem's title alone conjures up a Northern working-class set piece in a dismal chain pub/restaurant, and the first few lines sustain that expectation:

> All the men have comb-overs,
> bellies like cakes just baked,
> risen to roundness. The women tilt
> on their chairs, laughter faked ...

But the poem's speaker is confused by the women's behaviour. When all the men get up to get drinks from the bar, the women silently arrange the cutlery on the table and don't speak until the men return. Why? Ominously, the speaker plays footsie with a man,

> patience in his eyes who says *you can*

> *learn to love me*, ketchup
> on the hand that cups my chin,
> ketchup around his mouth,
> now hardening on my skin.

The last verb of the poem does some heavy lifting, darkly conjuring sexual violence and prepares us for the powerful, most arresting writing in the book, the central section 'How I Abandoned My Body To His Keeping', written in the voice of a survivor of a violent relationship. These poems confidently leave behind any self-consciousness of what they might be ABOUT and dig deeper into the urgent, struggling articulations of a victimized person. Still embedded in her consciousness is the tang of the perpetrator-partner's leather jacket, the threat in his hands. The language tries to disentangle itself from him, tries to gather a kind of agency in the act of coming to, of simultaneously realising and denying what is happening: 'it is sometimes painful / to have a knowing at your throat / that clever raven / but better than the alternative / something small and bruised / the raven knows most things / it remembers nothing / this is really about the trees / which saw it all' ('The Knowing'). This is powerful writing.

Much has been written of the ABOUT of Sarah Howe's lauded first book *Loop of Jade*, i.e., that Hong Kong-born, UK-raised-and-educated Howe is a person of 'mixed origin' (hated phrase! who isn't?) who writes of returning to some Chinese places of her mother's heritage. The beastly racist, sexist and ageist comments stirred up in some public fora after the book won the TS Eliot Prize were an unfortunate sideshow that temporarily detracted from the book's many merits. Indeed *Loop of Jade*'s title poem is a masterpiece of empathic imagination, a poem that brilliantly scores a daughter's conflicted recollections of a mother's 'non-native' voice and the mother's hesitating, recollecting voice in tender, lapidary measures:

> I can never know this place. Its scoop of rice in a chink-rimmed bowl, its
> daily thinning soup.

But to dwell only on the book's culturo-geographic ABOUT-ness is to miss the depth and breadth of its conceptual and technical complexities. (Note the mixed message carried by the word 'chink', the emphatic line break). Howe deploys a wide range of technical devices never for pyrotechnics, always for compositional appropriateness. She weighs words and their placement and poetic forms with inordinate care. The book's initial poem 'Mother's Jewellery Box', is written in spare triplets that formally represent the box's winged lids and central chamber and lyrically unfurl with a goldsmith's sense of precision:

> the twin lids
> of the black lacquer box
> open away ...

Howe is a scholar-poet with an etymologic, encyclopedic sensibility, hence Borges in the epigraph and a Borges list as the book's skeletal device, with poems titled for classifications of animals in the fictional *Celestial Emporium of Benevolent Animals* from (a) to (n) distributed throughout. The sonnet '(n) That from a long way off look like flies' is indicative of how, like a miniaturist, Howe can pack so much into fourteen lines, from incidental detail to pathos to knowing wit. The subject is a squashed midgie in her student Shakespeare, 'Two sheer wings, stilled mid-word / trace out a glyph in a strange alphabet', and Howe wonders of the bug, with a line from *Titus Andronicus*, the most violent of Shakespeare's plays, '*how, if that fly / had a father and a mother?*' Then she magicks the poem into the funny, mundane present,

> The way my father,
> in his affable moods, always thinks you
> want a gin and tonic too. I wonder
> if I should scrape her off with a tissue.

There is also a strong *imagiste* strain, from the 'In a Station of the Metro'-esque 'rain, *n.*' to a poem about Pound in the Pisan gorilla cage, to the placement of Chinese characters in the text à la the *Cantos*. Poems set in a life-drawing room and in a painter's studio, 'the oyster-crust / at the edge of an unscraped palette', reveal Howe's deep attraction to visuality, to art-making. In public talks, Howe has also drawn meaningful connections between her writings and some contemporary Chinese public art and performance works. There is so much intelligence and breadth here; I can't wait to read what Howe writes next.

Vahni Capildeo's *Measures of Expatriation*, her fifth full-length book, has been often and inaccurately banished to the ABOUT 'zona' as well: that it is 'about identity' or 'aftermath of Empire' always emphasising a geographical axis, in her case Trinidad (her birthplace), the UK (her university and adult-life-place), with sub-zonas of Iceland – Capildeo is a scholar of Old Norse – and Glasgow (a beloved city/culture). To describe Capildeo's book from these sorts of ABOUT perspectives is to gloss over one of her fundamental stances: that roots are twisted, tangled things, that *patria* and *expatria* are inventions forced by questions from outside the self:

> How was it that till questioned, till displaced in the attempt to answer, I had scarcely thought of myself as having a country, or indeed as having left a country? The answer lies peripherally in looming, in hinterland; primarily in the tongueless, palpitating interiority.
>
> – 'FIVE MEASURES OF EXPATRIATION: III GOING NOWHERE, GETTING SOMEWHERE'

Capildeo's book reminds me of conceptual-functional instruments of communication that artist Krzysztof Wodiczko designed in the 1990s for 'strangers' (immigrants, aliens, refugees) to wear in their new communities. Wodiczko's *Aegis: Equipment for a City of Strangers* (1999) is a backpack that has 'wings' – video screens that extend from the shoulders when the wearer wants to deploy a complex answer to 'the seemingly simple and well-meaning, but deeply insulting '"Where are you from?"', and 'can only be given in the form of a dialogue between two concurrently present images, and can never be achieved without revealing one's own contradictions'.[1] Capildeo's writing offers fluent, complex, elusive, authoritative answers to that unmaking question, 'Where are you from?'. She is anything but tight-lipped. Her flowing, agglutinate, searching, playful writing style is a refusal to be othered, a fearless exploration of her own 'palpating interiority'. Capildeo's writing IS.

The book, in its IS-ness, answers the poet's question posed to herself: 'What would I have called home, before I began creating home?' Capildeo stakes her claim decidedly: 'Language is my home, I say; not one particular language.' The brilliant poem 'Too Solid Flesh' excavates the shattering of self-coherence when one is upheaved from innate subjectivity to an object state: 'Being looked at, I was that unmade image.' This dispersion is far more than topographical. It's the dispersion of a person, a consciousness outside the bounds of her body, an eerie, floating intellect with a refusal to 'acquire density'. The poem is a frightening, courageous document written from the point of view of a disembodied speaker who can't be pinned down: 'Their question, "Where is she from?" in my very presence became, "Where is she?"'.

These are just small tastings from this sumptuous book. It's witty too. Capildeo sums up the beauty and brains issue faced by many an intelligent woman. At a dinner party, her speaker encounters an 'Armed Forces man' who thinks he can solve her problems, telling her 'essentially, I was the same as any woman, if we could put aside the intellect'. As if. The poet answers Armed Forces man with a declaration of the authority of her mind: 'Reading could fix me. It could be a way to acquire weight.'

Notes
1 At the time of going to print the website with this specific citation is offline (www.k-wodiczko.com/aegis-equipment-for-a-city-of-strangers). However, for further reference, see Wodiczko's lecture on his immigrant constructions: http://www.bu.edu/buniverse/view/?v=1lV8st9M

Kimberly Campanello

'FARM ANIMALS ...'

Farm animals, or a certain
valued ^do
species of dog, are better   Mahon Mary 11/04/1928 1 1/4 mts
treated than humans and
there is an urgent need to
review this whole system of
boarding out children who
by accident of birth have
have neither home nor

Kimberly Campanello

'WE CANNOT GUARANTEE ...'

we cannot guarantee
that the content or
'facilities' of the website
will always be current,
accurate or complete
moreover we cannot
guarantee that access to
the website won't be
interrupted   the
commission   of
investigation   into
mother and baby homes
and   certain   related
matters   reserves   the
right to remove, vary or
amend   any   of   the
content which appears
on its website at any
time and without prior

Fahey Mary Kate 04/05/1928 3 yrs

Kimberly Campanello

'I LIKE IT MUCH BETTER ...'

I like it much better just to read
this board because trying to get to
know what God wants takes an
awful lot of time and there is so
much to pray for. I leave Ireland to
St Patrick to take care of us. He

Note: *MOTHERBABYHOME* (zimZalla, 2017) is a 796-page book of poems
on St Mary's Mother and Baby Home in Tuam, which was run from
1926 to 1962 by the Bon Secours Sisters on behalf of the Irish state. The
location of the graves of the 796 children who died there is unknown,
though local knowledge points to a nearby field. An excavation of voices,
these poems are composed of text from archives and contemporary
sources related to the Home.

Luke Kennard

RED TAPE

Last night I dreamed you were trapped in a narrow wooden channel
and I couldn't reach you, although I could see the top of your
head and hear you crying. In the morning I found your icon of
St Moses the Ethiopian had fallen down the back of the dresser.
The ramifications are horrifying. I have turned myself in to the
police station on the mount.
Time to get the childish things down from the attic. Is the Book of
Life literally a book and could it fall on you because it hasn't
been appropriately fastened to a wall, because that's ridiculous.
A big glowing CGI book. All code. It's patronising.
We don't need it. When I was a metaphor I spoke in metaphors and
did metaphorical things, but now I am a metonym and have put
away metaphors. I wrestle metonyms on top of the metonymic
foothills in the night. My car is idling with its lights on and five
doors open, a metal flower in full bloom. The endlessly divisible
is easily dismissible: A thick mist of patchouli from a headshop;
The kind eyes of the Christian Union girl who tells you you're
going to Hell;
Form. I move the sofa, then the dresser, pick off the dust bunnies. I
can hear you.

Luke Kennard

AND ALL THE OTHER PUPPETS

The targeted adverts got better and better until there was no longer
      any product; pure eerie prescience.
The sound of a piano underwater.
What is this need to be adored by absolutely everyone which is felt
      by absolutely everyone. Some preening vanity which has its
      manifestation one way or another, has its way, and even then
      suspects some ulterior motive. Hopes to find worse in others.
Have you just trodden on a nectarine? (I had just trodden on a
      nectarine).
You know how she has made you want to write again? You could
      die of this.
That one sad thing which you know makes you ultimately unloveable.
      Speak it now in the following silence. Cue the strings. Cut the
      strings. How frightening everything is. I could be your surge
      protector. Or something.
Hell is every *Paris Review* at once. I think what I was trying to do here.
      I mean.

Joey Connolly

THIRD BALLAD
   – two versions of 'Ballade III' by Christine de Pizan

I.

And as Leander crossed that salted strait,
alive at his skin to the water, in all its
unsettled electrolytes, all craftless and concealed,
a disappearing small packet of risk, breathing her name
into his fearful shoulder with every
fifth stroke, her home on the snatched in-breath.
And as she waited, Hero, composed of that same, dark water:
      look how love orders the lover.

Across the sound – from which
so many have shouted – our little Leander pants
for old love, unsatisfactory and noble, parcelled inside
the unfolded carnation of heat his chest holds
against the near-freezing water. Against that passage:
raw chance, the violence of numbers, voltage, charts
and patterns, the hubris of analysis, weather-fronts: a storm.
      Foresight. See how love orders the lover.

Look how seeing preempts the gulf.
And Leander drowned himself in it, noble
and unsatisfactory. And Hero, in all things fit-for-purpose,
lost herself to it, too, at the same time as he,
if later. As this: one cause, one effect.
See this, poor etiolated lovers, at
the seafloor of love's furious cause:
      look at how love orders the lover. Look

and learn nothing. I beg you.
This ordering, this deluging myth-kitty; we crave it
overrule our cretin solitude: are desperate for it.

      Look at how love orders the lover.

II.

Always a line I told myself I'd never cross,
this retelling of the Greeks, a long game
I'm utterly without feeling for. And now (no hero, no claim
to heroism) I find you handing me the literal and I fold,
craftless and concealed in the face of
you, your mind, your body. Breathing the metre of it,
Medieval French to English. Parcelling something across.

Look how love orders the lover.

This sound, these English vowels I've made – if anything –
my home, I shout from them my hectors at the French.
Watch me struggle, craftless in the face of order.
Listen, Frenchy: the gap between our tongues
is just the blackest water, nothingy and unbreathable
with wordlessness, knowable at exactly and only those points at which
waves raise like scars from the skin
to catch that scattered, consonantal moonlight.

What survives the crossing? The correspondence
of two white corpses (*look how love …*)
pushed together by the tide of odds, these
devastated, idiolected lovers. Ten causes,
uncountable effects, a mess of want and
best guess, a sad seafloor of unthinkable love, everybody
just basically wanting to look good, everybody
just trying to write one good poem.
And to push it across, through the nasty insulation

of language, of the straight and the sound.
Don't stop. I'm sorry. Watch
for that washed-up body, white
and spoken with love.

Colette Bryce

IN DIFFERENT VOICES

Alice Oswald, *Falling Awake* (Cape Poetry, 2016), £10.
Denise Riley, *Say Something Back* (Picador Poetry, 2016), £9.99.

'In Berkshire somewhere 1970', begins the poem 'Aside' in Alice Oswald's new collection, 'I hid in a laurel bush outside a house, [...] pushed open / its oilskin flaps and settled down / in some kind of waiting room'. The experience depicted might be an inverse of Elizabeth Bishop's 'In the Waiting Room' where the horrified recognition of one's connection to the human race occurs, of being 'one of *them*'. The 'I' in Oswald's poem, conversely, merges with the twilit, 'hear-through' chamber – becomes 'too evergreen to answer' – in an hour that 'has not yet ended'. One of the most intriguing lyrics in the book, it reduces punctuation as it progresses, dispensing with the obstacle of initial caps while retaining the necessary pause of the full stop. The poem aligns to the right hand margin, not a new device by any means, but entirely suited to the sense of enclosure and screen between the speaker and (we assume) the suburban world.

The Bishopian specificity of place and date is unusual. If you were to open *Falling Awake* in the year 1970, in Berkshire or anywhere else, there would be little to alert you that it was written in the future. No direct contemporary reference would betray even the decade of publication. The lyrics here have a timeless quality in their engagement with the natural world and its processes, while the ancient world is superimposed on the Devon landscape like the shadows of clouds.

Man-made objects are alluded to occasionally (surgical gloves, a china serving dish), but none that would perplex our 1970s reader. When we read that 'walkers float / on the wings of their macs' ('A Drink from Cranmere Pool'), we are not referring to GPS on iPads, or Gore-Tex jackets on the hiking trails of Dartmoor, but to the rather quaint idea of the mackintosh, a word choice somehow in keeping with a pervading atmosphere of mid-twentieth-century diction. In this respect, a reader could forget that Oswald is successor, rather than contemporary, to Ted Hughes, an acknowledged presiding spirit in her work.

Hughes is invoked in the short lyric 'Fox', a slippery poem in which the famous midnight visitor is gendered female and then re-gendered, 'a woman with a man's voice / but no name'. The fox-fur alludes to Dionysus and his followers the Maenads, who in their fury ripped Orpheus to pieces and disposed of his head in the river Hebron. Thus, the next poem gives voice to the head, in a suitably drifting kind of form, using repetition, space and pause, and sounding a Beckettian note that recurs elsewhere:

        already forgetting who I am
        the water wears my mask   I call I call
        lying under its lashes like a glance
                        – 'SEVERED HEAD FLOATING DOWNRIVER'

'Flies', from which the book's title is drawn, raises the ghost of another
great American, the words 'stunned', 'trembling', and 'puzzlement' recalling the 'stumbling buzz' of Emily Dickinson's most chilling scenario.
The sheer pleasure to be had from the precision of Oswald's imagery can
be evidenced here:

        this is one of those wordy days
        when they drop from their winter quarters in the curtains
            and sizzle as they fall
        feeling like old cigarette butts called back to life
        blown from the surface of some charred world

The Dickinson echo is an early pointer to a central idea in the collection,
that of continuous consciousness; not only the head of Orpheus carrying
on its watery thought process, but a swan departing its own corpse with
mild surprise, 'leaving her life and all its tools / with their rusty juices
trickling back to the river' ('Swan'). This is taken further in the superb
lyric 'Body' where the bewildered dead are attempting steps below a 'thin
partition', while above ground a badger runs through the instant of its own
death and goes 'on running along the hedge and into the earth again /
trembling'.
    In 'Village', slightly menacing character portraits accrue, giving the
lie to any notion of a rural idyll. The repetition of banal fillers – 'this is
god's honest truth', 'say what you like' – weave in and out of a nervy
surface chatter. The phrase 'not many of us left' underlines the sense of
endgame, a Beckettian cast hanging on, fearful gossip playing over on a
loop. The distinct energy of the piece is a reminder of Oswald's consider-
able dramatic talent that infused her book-length poems *Dart* (2002) and
A Sleepwalk on the Severn (2009).
    The agony of endgame reaches its apotheosis in the myth of Tithonus,
lover of the Dawn, whose gift of eternal life without youth becomes the
ultimate 'I can't go on, I'll go on'. Originally commissioned by the South-
bank Centre, 'Tithonus' is essentially a script for performance, pinned
typographically to a marginal timeline of 46 minutes, each utterance cued
to the very second. Its enactment of the dawn wholly inhabits the hour
that 'has not yet ended' of 'Aside', and indeed the collection does not
(cannot?) conclude, but fades out, as the ink disappears by degrees on the
last page.
    Oswald has spoken about her quest for the lightness of the oral poets,
and of the rhythmic soundscape being central to her enterprise. What a

reader takes away, however, more than this, is the consistent brilliance of her imagery, the meticulous observations out of which she fashions the bright likenesses of her similes and metaphors. These are what go on fizzing in the mind long after the printed page is set aside.

> There's no specific noun for a parent of a dead child; nothing like the terms for other losses such as 'orphan' or 'widower'. No single word exists, either, for an 'adult child' – an awkward phrase which could suggest a large floppy-limbed doll. For such a historically frequent condition as outliving your own child, the entire vocabulary is curiously thin.

The above quotation is from Denise Riley's 2012 essay *Time Lived, Without Its Flow*, a meditation on bereavement that could stand as a companion piece to the poems in her extraordinary new collection. Outliving one's own child is the dread subject of *Say Something Back*: the atemporality of the aftermath, and an enduring sense of unreality – that the loved one is simply 'away', even if away for one's 'remaining lifetime'.

Riley's taut lyrics circle around the fact of this loss, the voice by turns self-mocking, haunted, intimate, wise. The twenty short lyrics of 'A Part Song' wrestle with the question of poetry's purpose. As the love poem's function is to woo, the elegy aspires to recall in both meanings of the word; in one, always destined to fail. 'Art is born of humiliation', wrote Auden, and Riley likewise has noted the lyric's roots in shame, the shame here being the parental sense of failure: *'What is the first duty of a mother to a child? / At least to keep the wretched thing alive'*. The lyric impulse itself comes under scrutiny as the speaker thumbs through elegiac conventions, like bargaining chips to 'extort' a reply, only to undermine or reject them:

> I can't get sold on reincarnating you
> As those bloody 'gentle showers of rain'
> Or in 'fields of ripening grain' – oooh
> Anodyne ...

'She do the bereaved in different voices' comments the poem, à la Eliot, but while the posture changes, it is the address rather that seems to shift: now to the reader, now to a beleaguered self, but mostly to the 'Strangely unresponsive son' towards whom the speaker directs all the persuasion of her art:

> It's all a resurrection song.
> Would it ever be got right
> The dead could rush home
> Keen to press their chinos.

Carol Ann Duffy, in her poem 'Premonitions', reverses time to resurrect the lost mother through skill in language alone, an Orphic enterprise achieving a semblance of consolation within the parameters of the poem. *Say Something Back* confronts the failure of poetry ever to effect this 'undoing'. It moves through the various rooms of bereavement, disbelief, stasis, catastrophic thinking, even trying exasperated parental imperative: 'Oh my dead son you daft bugger / This is one glum mum. Come home I tell you' ('A Part Song').

WS Graham provides the book's epigraph, and the affinity with Graham's late style is strong. There is a new directness in Riley's approach, a clarity of address, and sometimes a risky simplicity that always pays off. Black humour, irony and bathos mitigate against the gravitational pull of the material, but the poems are extremely moving for all of that. A suitably muscular poem, 'Cardiomyopathy', scrutinizes the recorded cause of death:

> I'm sounding
> too forensic? – but you'll go on with your dead,
> go as far as you can; that's why my imagination
> wouldn't wait outside the morgue, but burst in
> to half-anaesthetise itself with knowing ...

Two further sequences balance out the middle and the end of the collection. While 'The patient who had no insides' may exhibit a few symptoms of commissionitis, it also delivers some outstanding Riley lines: 'That piece of ambient meat I am eats meaty me all up'; 'Googling / Fulfils the nineteenth century's dream of ardent enquiry'.

It is not only the bereaved that 'she do' in different voices, but the dead also. In 'A gramophone on the subject', marking the centenary of the First World War, the fallen conscripts speak from their muddled graves, alongside an exhumation squad, and finally the voice of the everymother, struggling to make sense of her loss:

> I never could grasp human absence.
> It always escaped me, the real name
>
> of this unfathomable simplest thing.
> It's his hands I remember the most.

In her essay, Riley wrote of searching for texts that addressed the 'arrested time' of bereavement, only to discover a literary absence. 'If there's a book that you want to read, but it hasn't been written yet, then you must write it', Toni Morrison once advised. In *Say Something Back,* Riley has done precisely that, her incisive lyrics cutting through the silence around this universal experience. These are poems that advance our literature of bereavement, that offer no easy consolations, but lucidly and artfully articulate the condition of that loss.

Igor Klikovac

GRATITUDE TO BIG CITIES

Those days when all pages are empty
are best given to running. Knowing your own name
is less important if the streets are long, and – better still –
freshly scrubbed by rain. Then it looks like you're jumping
from one façade to another, above the outstretched necks
and open windows, and that alone already feels like
an improvement. Under the coloured canopies, through
the courtyards of tiny churches, over the pedestrian bridges
that cross no water; through the sleepy eyes of rear-mirrors,
from shop-window to shop-window, like a rambling thought.
Underneath you, the specially designed soles squeal,
and manhole covers rattle with the rhythm of images
barely catching up with their own mortality statistics ...
The problem of the cracked self, thus reduced to a simple
breathing exercise, at the end simply solves itself, like
a common cold. When finally you open your eyes,
the world is again joined up by words, the light thread
which meanders through the scenery like yellow stitching
in a pair of blue-jeans, and the woman taking a jumper
from a washing-line and smelling it, while behind her
in the distance a weather balloon rises, is already
surrounded by that insatiable whiteness, the one
which never lets out what it once swallowed.

– translated by **Igor Klikovac** and **John McAuliffe**

Igor Klikovac

RATS' DECISION

Dogs were slowly going rabid; cats, it was assumed,
had simply walked out. Bluebottles had a field day.
You want to see what rats are doing, a neighbour said,
if they stay it'll be bad, but it's a no-hoper if they leave.
So we played chess and waited for the sign, until
one day the others told me he'd left too, the rat-expert.

Months later, with swallows, I was on my way out
when I saw a forgotten classmate on the enemy checkpoint
go through people's papers, and thought stupidly: it's true,
everyone will have a story about the war. A borrowed name
in the pocket, my own in the coat's lining, I started praying
to the God of Rats that this doesn't become mine.

– translated by **Igor Klikovac** and **John McAuliffe**

Evan Jones

HIDDEN
– after CP Cavafy

From all I did and all I said,
don't hope to learn who once I was.
There were restrictions which affected
how I lived and how I behaved.
There were restrictions which forbade
speaking the way I wanted to.
My most intimate obsessions,
and my most private writings –
only these can reveal my self.
But maybe, learning about me
isn't worth such effort, such thought.
One day – in a world more perfect –
another similar to me
will appear, and he will be free.

Rebecca Watts

ECONOMICS

Everything comes down to numbers in the end.

This morning a blackbird woke me up; five swans in formation
trailed their silver chevrons upriver, unbothered by
the heron's slow torpedo; three horses in maroon jackets stood
mystified by their own breath. A greenfinch and thirty-nine
cows patterned the field; twin black labs trotted through
the long grass, jingling, and unearthed a compact of magpies.
I didn't count the dandelion clocks, there were so many.

You ask me would I move to the city to be with you.
I'm telling you what I saw; you can do the maths.

Simon Armitage

POOR OLD SOUL

'You'll enjoy it,' I say, when the carer arrives
and wants to wheel him to the park. I watch him
puzzling with the leather buttons
on his favourite coat, fingers like sticks of chalk.

Coming home from a week abroad I find him
hunched and skeletal under a pile of clothes,
a Saxon king unearthed in a ditch.
'I ran out of biscuits,' he says,

'and the telly's on – I couldn't make it stop.'
When I throw back the curtains, morning
bursts like a water balloon before he can rig up
his tatty umbrella of epidermis and bone.

Simon Armitage

OCTOBER

All day trimming branches and leaves, the homeowner
sweeping the summer into a green heap;
all evening minding the flames,
inhaling the incense of smouldering laurel and pine.

Or careering home from school down Dog Shit Lane
between graves and allotments,
past the old churchwarden propped on a rake
in a standing sleep, bent over a fire
of cut flowers and sympathy cards and wreaths.

Bernard O'Donoghue

GETTING ON WITH LIFE

Derek Mahon, *New Selected Poems* (The Gallery Press / Faber and Faber, 2016), €13.90.

Derek Mahon's *New Collected Poems*, published by Gallery in 2011, claimed 'to bring together, in a new form, the poems the author wishes to preserve from the work of half a century', which sounded – at least for the time being – like a conclusive resolution of the canon of a poet which had been extremely difficult to finalise. Now, five years later, comes this corresponding *New Selected* in which, it tells us, 'all but two of these poems appear, some in slightly different versions' in that 2011 *Collected*. It is the fifth Selected, after *Poems 1962-1978* from Oxford University Press, a volume which Mahon wanted to disavow as he moved from Oxford University Press to single publication by Gallery. There were two Penguin Selecteds, in 1991 in conjunction with Gallery, and in 2000. But it sounds as if this Gallery-Faber collaboration is intended to have the same kind of *imprimatur* as the 2011 *Collected*. Its publication, then, is a highly significant moment.

Mahon's career has been rather crudely divided into two major periods, often controversially described (in much the same way as Geoffrey Hill's). The first period, which has received universal acclaim, featured a steadily appearing series of slim volumes of lyric poems, from *Night-Crossing* (1968) to *The Hunt by Night* (1982), the last OUP single volume. Though there were several significant interim publications after that, there was no full-length volume between 1982 and the publication of *The Hudson Letter*, a very different kind of book, in 1995. *The Hudson Letter* was a series of 18 longer poems, from 28 to 70 lines, in a freer, more conversational tone, very different from the tight, elegant forms of the early lyrics, but linking to the friendly style of the shorter *Yaddo Letter*, written from America to his children ('you guys') in 1992. The change of style was confirmed by the appearance in 1997 of *The Yellow Book*, 19 poems in a similarly free form. So the second period, a more critically contested one, extends from 1992 onwards. The blurb on the back of the *New Selected* proposes a third period, 'the flowering of his late style', drawing on the poems published since *The Yellow Book*. But what has now been achieved, I think, by the current *Collected* and *Selected* is a convincing stabilisation of Mahon's oeuvre, particularly in softening the starkness of the divisions between the first two periods.

There is a third volume to be incorporated into the complete poetic canon of Mahon, though. Hugh Haughton noted in 2002 that *The Hudson Letter* and *The Yellow Book* 'integrate translation into his own work', something that was reinforced by the appearance four years later of *Adapta-tions*, Mahon's volume of translations and versions. The design of the new book makes it unmistakably a companion to *Adaptations,* with the same John Minihan picture of the poet on the back and a similar placing of an abstract painting on the front. These books are meant to go together, completing a set.

There are some remaining complications of reference. The whole of *The Hudson Letter* is included in the 2011 *Collected* and nearly all of *The Yellow Book,* though with some changes and deletions. But they are not so easy to find there, because *The Hudson Letter* appeared as *New York Time*, and *The Yellow Book* as *Decadence*. Mahon is often compared to Wordsworth and Auden as poets who revised their poems substantially, and, in the view of some readers, not always for the better. Haughton's 'Inventory of Poems' in his magisterial 2007 *The Poetry of Derek Mahon* resolved the complications of nomenclature up to that point. It is still valuable, but it is keyed into the 1999 *Collected* so it is overtaken by the appearance of the later *Collected* and now the *Selected*. What Haughton called Mahon's 'cunningly contrived canonical reshaping' still continues.

The most striking advantage of the organization of the *New Selected* is that some of the longer, more discursive poems of the later periods are incorporated into the whole of the corpus without any evident sense of disruption or departure, so it is interesting to ponder how the poems from *The Hudson Letter* (these are headed 'from *New York Time*') and the two from *The Yellow Book* (headed 'from *Decadence*') were chosen. The second of the two from *The Yellow Book,* Mahon's desolately moving and often misrepresented elegy for his mother, 'A Bangor Requiem' (earlier 'Death in Bangor'), links more naturally with the great short poem 'Ghosts' (originally 'Siren', from *Harbour Lights* in 2005) which follows it now, beginning:

> We live the lives our parents never knew
> when they sang 'Come Back to Sorrento'.

Mahon, 'a strange child with a taste for verse' ('Courtyards in Delft'), has often been compared to Louis MacNeice, whom he greatly admires. In fact it is possible to view the third phase of Mahon's as a development like MacNeice's admired late flowering with the poems of *The Burning Perch* and other great lyrics. Mahon too has had a post-period-two flower-ing with poems like 'Ghosts', and the *New Selected* reflects it well. There are two poems later than the 2011 *Collected*, one of which, 'Palinurus', is a masterpiece, comparable to MacNeice's late classical lyrics such as 'Thalassa'. It is an example of a poetic form that Mahon does exceptionally well, which is to follow closely the narrative contours of a received story or earlier poem to apply to a new situation which runs parallel to it: the word 'Adaptations', applied to his translations, fits it well. A prototype of such poems perhaps is Tennyson's 'Ulysses'. Mahon's poem questions what caused the helmsman Palinurus to fall to his death – a blackout, Juno's divine intervention, or loss of faith in Aeneas – but in any case the outcome fits Mahon's condition very well:

> wanting no more of the great expedition
> I chose obscurity and isolation –
> childish perhaps, but there you are.
> On an unfriendly, now a friendly shore ...

This version of Palinurus' escape fits Mahon's withdrawal to Kinsale wittily (though some critics, notably Peter McDonald, would feel that Coriolanus might be a better figure for it). Another striking example of this kind of remoulding of a received text or episode survives into the *New Selected*, 'The Widow of Kinsale', a brilliant reworking of the Old Irish 'Cailleach Beara' as an ageing Anglo-Irish lady, driving over in her 'olive vintage Rover / to Bantry or even Dingle', or preferring to 're-read for ever / the novels of William Trevor, / that lovely man'. It is a twinkling knitting together of the Gaelic bardic tradition with the world of Elizabeth Bowen or Molly Keane or JG Farrell.

So what are we to make of Mahon as a whole, on the basis of this resolving *Selected*? The admired early poems are pretty severely sifted (after all, 124 pages is an exacting allowance for this substantial corpus), but the effect of this is to make the survivors seem all the more outstanding. The 54 pages here, from the mock-Sophoclean 'Glengormley' to the painful memoir of 'Dawn at St Patrick's', is an extraordinarily sustained body of powerful and memorable poems; but that was to be expected. Mahon used occasionally to suffer the critical fate that Elizabeth Bishop lamented with her 'Fish' poem – universal association with a single work, a fate which of course she richly overcame latterly. Mahon's corresponding admired albatross is 'A Disused Shed in Co. Wexford' which, like Bishop's poem, is now just a *primus inter pares* of outstanding work. The poem 'Rain', the last of the four 'from *New York Time*' (*The Hudson Letter*) included here, ends with a clear allusion to the fate of the mushrooms in that poem, recognizing a Mahon motif:

> We have been too long in the cold. – Take us in; Take us in!

Other Mahon subjects are emphasized by selecting poems for their thematic echoes. His interest in visual art remains prominent in all the periods; two of the volumes are named from paintings but a positive commitment to art in general is something Mahon has always been associated with: his range of reference is very wide, in music (Mozart, Schubert, Dvořák), philosophy (Heraclitus, Lucretius, Nietzsche), and literature (Montaigne, Brecht, Pliny, Voznesensky). But it is not cosmopolitanism for the sake of it; there is no sense of dry learning. Hugh Haughton said acutely that Mahon also has 'a unique respect for obsolete modernity', so the wonders of man in Sophocles are replaced by terrier-taming, hedge-trimming and 'the principle of the watering can'. It sounds more like Flann O'Brien than Greek tragedy. And this comic modernity in Mahon has been enhanced by the move in a stylistic discursive direction.

It is a long time since Mahon (or his persona) in *The Snow Party* in 1975 said he was 'through with history' ('The Last of the Fire Kings'). One of the striking things in the later poems is his frequent cross-reference to contemporary history. This is very noticeable in the poem with which he ends both the *Collected* and the *Selected*, 'Dreams of a Summer Night'. After an arty start with *A Midsummer Night's Dream*, Bergman and the Mozart Oboe concerto as the sun sets over the Bandon river, the poet reflects on the past gold rush and the slump, wondering if we can forget about market forces:

Can we relax now and get on with life?

It may not be as momentous as Treblinka and Pompeii, but it allows the books, and the whole poetic assembly, to end with a hard-earned reconciliation, awaiting 'the daylight we were born to love ... the lives we live'. It is a surprising (and of course still provisional) positive ending. But nobody will begrudge it at the end of a glorious body of work.

Medbh McGuckian

THE SNOWFALL ROOM

The mesmerizing weather
Has a very rich yellowing
Like the sky over Verdun
And Railway Hollow Wood.

Feet over leaves in the thin
Remnant of air
Try to account
For the fallen leaves

Or what happened
To our promised moon –
Five great dyings
Blurring their stars together.

The change of a certain
Sound makes the star
More and more
Peachlike, the earth

Would find itself
Inside a star,
The heart of a star.
The starlanes littered

With the eyes of stars,
But fewer blue-white
Stars. Archaic sparrows
Probe the crowded starfields

Of the flying angel
Painter, whose musical
Salvation is how to find the
North, to touch her leaves.

Dom Bury

HIRAETH

> *A homesickness for a home to which you cannot return,*
> *the nostalgia, the yearning, the grief for the lost places of your past.*
> — Welsh word for which there is no direct English translation

The town tonight is like a little scuttled ship; the river closed
with ice and each road, each roof, each room frost closeted.

And still in spite of this, in spite of snow the roses push up blade
by blade to shake out their small white fires, and will not close.

And I must confess this stirs in me another road, another
ice-clutched path which, despite the winter, would not close.

Further down it I have walked, past the harbour locked into the hills
to where the sea turns in its sleep, its one white eye half-closed.

And though I name this home I feel it as a roof stripped off –
a scab, an old wound which, despite the years, will still not close.

And still I cannot say which map, which scroll of sky I'd used then
to guide me back, or which alternate life I'd then had to close.

And though it moves in me still; the sea, I know, I know I can't return
to that same shore the tide, that time has now dragged closed.

Lani O'Hanlon

THE CHERRY BLOSSOMS WERE PURPLE THERE
 – for John

That autumn, Australian spring,
in the forest where we camped
the trees were full of coloured birds
with strange cries and calls
and mossies that bit the legs off you.

In the ocean, waves came in sideways
across our hips and there was a rip
that could drag you out to sea,
indigo jelly fish with ferocious stings.

We ate mangoes for breakfast,
raisin toast and coffee in the café,
tame parrots, white and green and pink,
croaked helloo helloo.

Every evening we walked through the woods.
There, we said, looking up at the dozy koalas.
Tea-tree and Eucalyptus drip dripped
their juices into the lake,
bark peeled and shed itself,
we hung our clothes from the branches.

Matt Howard

CROME
v.

to cast a tool of ash and hooked iron

to take care in boots at the edge of standing water

to throw from the shoulder, then heave from the lumbar spine

to clear a dyke of leaf-fall and slub from the past three decades or further

to feel a suck and pop of sedge-roots tearing from bog

to spit splash-back of festered water from one's lips

to wretch one's balance of vows and curses where no one else is listening

to imagine a cut of clearer water

to haul deeper with long-draw tines

to blister then callus both hands in unfavourable conditions

to consider the phased wing-strokes of dragonflies

to listen to the short, descending arc of willow warbler song whilst working

to see sunlight on the nodes of a Norfolk hawker's forewing

to act with the whole body and mean it

Mary O'Donnell

THOSE PROSTITUTES IN CUBA

They were like two kittens, he said,
snuggling up to him,
they were fun and they liked him.

I thought – against my own sex – how
enviable his freedom to fall in
with such company, then breakfast

with them afterwards, heartily, admiring
their health, their strong teeth, that
vitality. It could never happen

to a woman my age, two tiger men
who would not wound, the three of us
so human in a dusky room, sunlight

stealing through the slats in colours
from Matisse, the riotous world
within and without.

Joseph Woods

TIDING US OVER

Grace Wells, *Fur* (Dedalus Press, 2015), €12.50.
Michelle O'Sullivan, *The Flower and the Frozen Sea* (The Gallery Press, 2015), €11.95.
Aideen Henry, *Slow Bruise* (Salmon Poetry, 2015), €12.

Fur is Grace Wells's second poetry book and is endorsed by Thomas McCarthy, who speaks of Wells's elegance, style and sense of purpose. This is entirely apt, while his mention of the 'feast of poetry' refers, I think, to this book's engagingly optimistic and redemptive contents. Wells's stance is described in the first poem, set on Achill Island, where the poet is energised by her environment (and the bounty of the Heinrich Böll cottage), and on her bike, concludes:

> I must warn you not to go there
>
> unless you are able for that sea wind,
> unless you are ready to change your life.

That riff on Rilke sets the tone, and over the five sections of the book there's an exploration of the natural world, via 'Animal Encounters' and 'Becoming Human' to a concluding 'Cornucopia'. Underlying these explorations lies something of a meditation on what each of us carries beneath our skin, or beneath the *Fur* of the title; and also in part an allusion to the 'crane bag' – the myth, not the eponymous literary journal. I didn't quite follow this theme, further elaborated in the Notes, but was moved by the many fine poems and their *joie de vivre* – or perhaps *joie de la poésie* – which is all too rare, these days.

Wells's reach and range in poetry is wide and diverse, exploring form and subject matter, and elegantly manipulating material like 'The Long Corridor' (after Dennis O'Driscoll), where she writes a version of his poem and yet his own absence is marked within its corridors. 'Poem for Tennessee Williams' is an achieved 'biopoem', focusing on Williams' failed first play, and creating a current response whereby the poet walks in on the playwright's space:

> I aim to slip into your low lit room.
> I plan to leave some bank notes
> on your dresser. I want to thank you
> for lines you are yet to write.
> I want to tide you over.

In other hands this could be incongruous, but done with empathy and delicacy, it works. Elsewhere in a poem addressed to Holdridge of 'Holdridge's toad' fame (I hadn't heard of it either), the poem starts off with the absurdity of animals named after people or their 'discoverers'. In this case the toad is extinct, and possibly Holdridge is also, but then the poem widens to become an eloquent indictment of species and extinction. Among the many excellent poems in the latter sections, Wells closes one ('I Thought I Was Done with Those Poems') with the simple phrase 'sensate on the earth'; it could be a subtitle to *Fur*, a book that enlarges the possibilities of poetry.

Michelle O'Sullivan's *The Flower and the Frozen Sea* comes with a kind of pre-accolade, a Poetry Book Society Recommendation – and like all three books reviewed here, it's the writer's second collection. I've often wondered whether people buy PBS Recommendations in the way that some might buy the Man Booker shortlist?

Both the title, perhaps referring to the Frozen Sea of Okhotsk, and the cover illustration of a Japanese woman peering out from a screen, had me thinking this was a book themed on Japan. There's also a poem with a Japanese title but I think the primary 'Japanese' effect here is an incredibly keen observation of the natural world, as reflected in Japan's ancient poetry, and to some extent in ours, especially reaching back to the early scribe-monks and their pure and sparse marginalia.

Stylistically, O'Sullivan has much of this: short intense lyrics of brief lines and invariably brief poems, drawing more contemporaneously on the work of Moya Cannon, Joan McBreen or Seán Lysaght. Nature (O'Sullivan's locale is in Co Mayo) is her inspiration, and her occasions for poems are often at the beginning or at the end of the day. 'Partial', a poem which opens the book, closes on this third stanza:

> One curtain is pulled aside,
> the other still drawn.
> For the time being
> this is the light we're living by.

This is simple, revelatory and surprising, but it also indicates the quietude this poet invokes. Here's the close of day, in 'Elements':

> Almost dark.
> One hand reaches for the hasp and stays,
> the stiff heart
> turns on a question.

'Elements' is also interesting because it's typical of O'Sullivan's work as a poet of the natural world, but not necessarily as a naturalist poet: her approach is painterly, imagistic, obsessively adumbrating and describing, to get it right. In 'Januaries', there is the rather wonderful phrase 'white clouds working / themselves loose', and later the 'glide of goldfinches' can be forgiven – it's nicely alliterative, but I'm not sure finches actually glide. Some of the poems trespass into anthropomorphic or personification terrain (as do some of Grace Wells's poems), but none jar.

Throughout this collection there is an adherence to what the poet knows well, a consistency in delivering precise imagery in the short form and fragment. One minor quibble might be a certain repetition: the river, the sky (or clouds or stars), and trees – some or all of these are mentioned in almost every poem. That said, there are no quotas in poetry and nothing wrong with a field study.

Philip Larkin once said that 'one doesn't really choose the kind of poetry one writes. One writes the kind of poetry one has to write.' This is very clear in O'Sullivan's meditations on the river Moy and her corner of Mayo – though other locations are invoked and imagined – Orkney, Kinsale and rural Australia. In the final poem, 'Station', the 'gates of the city' are tantalisingly recalled, and whichever direction O'Sullivan takes next can only be interesting.

Slow Bruise, Aideen Henry's second book, charts, according to its blurb, emotion 'intensely felt yet tamed, so that the poems are cool and palatable and yet red hot with feeling'. Structured in three parts, the book is interleaved with life drawings by Mary Avril Gillan and bound in a muted cover of yellow and blue. The book certainly appears as a cohesive structure, where the second part will (again, according to the blurb) 'reveal all facets of romantic entanglement from their tentative beginnings, on into the sensuous, finally reaching the forensic brutality of a relationship ended, combining unashamed desolation with a dignified grappling with grief'. It's a tall order or prescription (the poet is a physician) to follow, and there's also an undercurrent of Irish translations and Hiberno-English expressions throughout.

Going by the dedications of some of these poems, Henry clearly has an interesting literary background and heritage. In a poem recalling her father ('Warming-Down') they revisit Inishbofin, the island of his youth:

> The first inkling of the wind-down,
> our stertorous walk.

The poem is nicely paced and interfaced with three lines of his native Irish. In 'Hiberno-English', Henry carefully delineates a bachelor-turned-father who 'always scalded the teapot for one' and continued to do so as his family grew up. Henry's strengths in this book tend toward narratives and it comes as no surprise that she has already published a collection of short stories with Arlen House, *Hugging Thistles* (2013). A number of poems respond to paintings and painters; in 'A Shorthand of Sensation', which, according to the epigraph, was how Francis Bacon described images, Henry focuses on actions:

> In the unconscious things people do
> they give themselves away;
>
> [...]
>
> inhaling slowly
> before turning a door knob,
>
> [...]
>
> repeating a story
> with the same voice inflexion at the turn

Slow Bruise, while not quite living up to its blurb, has some fine poems, though occasionally, in describing emotions ('Extraction', 'Moonless'), there's a tendency toward abstraction. However, in other poems Henry makes interesting use of medical terminology. It made me recall what the late Dannie Abse (also a poet-physician) said of a particular poem at a workshop in Galway some years ago: 'It's all there, just some adipose tissue needs to be removed.'

John McDonald

HAIKU

souch throuch
the abbey ruinage
... chauntin

leoithne trí
fhothrach na mainistreach
... cantaireacht

auld bull meditatin –
sin
on's pisle

 seantarbh ag machnamh ...
an ghrian
ar a bhod

armistice day –
leaves fawin
i thair millions

 lá sos cogaidh ...
duilleoga ag titim
ina milliúin

deid bawdrons
amang the leaves
... curlt up

 cat marbh
i measc na nduilleog
... cuachta suas

hallae e'en –
rackets smuir oot
the sterns

oíche shamhna ...
folaíonn tinte ealaíne
na réaltaí

i the burn
the monie-colourt clints
o hairst

sa tsruthán
carraigeacha ildaite
an fhómhair

on the boolin green
craws'r stoorin efter
a maw

ar an bhfaiche bollaí
préacháin sa tóir
ar fhaoileán

on a cloody day
yin straik o blae
... kingfisher

lá scamallach
stríoc ghorm amháin
... cruidín

hallae e'en –
pumpkin bree the day
pumpkin bree the morn

oíche shamhna –
anraith puimcín inniu
anraith puimcín amárach

'Laughing' by **Sven Sandberg**, 2016
Oil on canvas, 60 x 45.5cm
See **http://svensandberg.com**

The images in this issue consist of recent work from shortlisted and winning artists
from the RDS Visual Arts Awards 2016

Video still from the installation 'Limitless' by **Aoife Dunne**, 2016
See www.aoifedunne.com

'Dr. Nadia Kelbova' by **Justyna Kielbowicz**, 2016
Photograph shows one of the experiments of Dr. Nadia Kelbova and
   her Psychotronic Weapon Deflector
See http://justynakielbowicz.com

'Wanderer' by **Jane Rainey**, 2016
Oil on canvas, 120 x 150cm
See http://janeraineyart.com

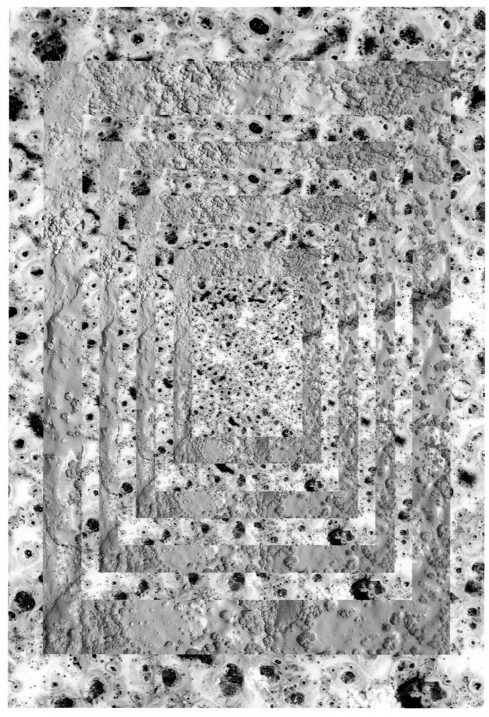

'The Lament of the Jade Phoenix' by **Michelle Hall**, 2016
Rotated still from 26-minute digital video
See http://michellehall.ie/

sweet peas
sclimin
the jyle palin

 piseanna cumhra
fál an phríosúin acu
á dhreapadh

i the doctor's surgery
a paulm tree
... deein

in íoclann an dochtúra
crann pailme
... ag fáil bháis

– transcreation from the Scots by **Gabriel Rosenstock**

Doireann Ní Ghríofa

AIBREÁN, 1912

Ar a shlí chuig suíomh an longbháite,
chonaic an Captaen de Carteret an cnoc oighir úd
trína dhéshúiligh. Ba léir go raibh an dochar déanta
cheana féin, an fhianaise soiléir:

stríoc fhada dhearg ar imeall an chnoic bháin,
scréach i bpéint.
B'in an marc a scaoil an scéal don Chaptaen,
chomh soiléir le teacht dheirge an dá néal

le breacadh an lae. Bhí an cnoc oighir mar a bheadh
laoch éigin as finscéal, fámaire fir tar éis treasruathar,
ag bacadaíl leis go himeall pháirc an áir, le scairt fola
óna thaobh, áit ar buaileadh é le rinn claímh, agus

le gach sleaschéim agus leathchéim, an laoch ard
ag claochlú, ag lagú. Chomh hársa
leis na sean-déithe, saolaíodh an sliabh oighir sin
le réim farónna na hÉigipte. Ginte sa Ghraonlainn

de chríonsneachta is oighear, scortha ó ghreim a mháthar-
oighearshruth chuig lapadaíl fhuar thaoidí an Aigéin Artaigh,
sceitheadh é, scaoileadh le sruth, go dtí an oíche gur chas sé
ar an long. Greadadh in éadan a chéile iad, ach lean sé

ar a shlí gan breathnú siar. Laistigh de chúpla bliain,
bhí seisean imithe leis, gan fágtha ina dhiaidh
ach spreachall fionnuisce breac le móilíní péinte
dearga scaipthe, scaoilte i sáile an aigéin.

Deirtear nach ann do uisce nua, go bhfuil an t-uisce
céanna de shíor ar fhéith-bhogadh timpeall orainn: ag leá,
ag reo, ag imeacht go haer, cosúil leis na héin, cosúil
linn féin, ár n-anam de shíor ag rince idir talamh is spéir.

Doireann Ní Ghríofa

ON GCRANN SILÍNÍ, LEÁNN NA PEITIL INA GCEANN AGUS INA GCEANN

Filleann an tseanbhean béal dorais arís
i mbrothall mheán lae, gan uirthi an babhta seo
ach gúna oíche agus bráisléad ospidéil. Suas-síos

an tsráid léi ag rámhaille léi. Cloisim an fear ag
uimhir a 3 – *Cuir glaoch ar na Gardaí, a Mháire,*
tá sí ar ais, an créatúr, tá sí ar strae ón ospidéal arís.

Siar is aniar léi, idir béicíl is cogarnaí. Síneann sí méar
chugainn ina nduine agus ina nduine, ag scréachaíl
go bhfuilimid go léir *i mbaol, i mbaol!*

Deir sí gur taibhsíodh di ár dtodhchaí,
oighearshruthanna ag leá, farraigí ag ardú!
Deir sí gur gá dúinn ár ngasúir a bhailiú láithreach

agus *éalú, éalú!* Ritheann sí ó dhoras go doras
ag béicíl *Imígí, imígí! Deifrígí, deifrígí!* go dtí
go dtagann an t-otharcharr arís. Ní fhágann a guth

ach macalla gairid ina diaidh. Tá sí sábháilte
anois, le beirt bhanaltra láidre dorn ar uilleann léi,
á hiompar ar ais chuig Barda na Néaltrú Seanaoise,

áit a suífidh sí arís i gcathaoir bhog os comhair
na teilifíse. Iompóidh sí a haghaidh ó réamhaisnéis
na haimsire, agus breathnóidh sí uaithi ar na crainn

silíní sa ghairdín, na peitil bhándearga a chlaochlaíonn
an cosán ina chiumhais tais tim. Ó ghéaga na gcrann,
feicfidh sí bláthanna ag titim agus ag titim.

Richard Hayes

HEARTS ALIGHT

Mary O'Donnell, *Those April Fevers* (Arc Publications, 2015), £9.99.
Gerry Murphy, *Muse* (Dedalus Press, 2015), €11.50.
Sara Berkeley Tolchin, *What Just Happened* (The Gallery Press, 2015), €11.95.

Those April Fevers is Mary O'Donnell's seventh collection. She is also a published novelist, short-story writer and a radio broadcaster. As one might expect of a writer with such experience, and with a history of achievement, the poems in *Those April Fevers* are confident intellectually and formally. In 'The Artists are Sleeping', she writes:

> Only the poets never truly sleep,
> restless in REM, the sieves of their imaginations
> still sifting language from muddy waters.
>
> They lie prone on pillows of stone,
> bardic to the last, unable to forsake
> the fever and fret, circadian rhythms ill-tuned
>
> for orderly living.

O'Donnell's gifts enable her imagination to be restless without appearing confused or ill at ease. A long poem, 'An Irish Lexicon', exemplifies that restlessness – the poem is a *Canto* for our times, a rich, ambitious, powerful rag-bag. O'Donnell's is indeed a bardic voice, and there are poems here addressed to the world as well as poems to do with more personal things. Or, indeed, poems that bring together the political and the personal, like the wonderfully titled 'On Fitzwilliam, after a budget'. O'Donnell recalls the recession of the 1980s. Now, thirty years later, she writes angrily, 'the carcass-rippers maul again, / money-lenders scatter'. And yet,

> ... like us, that couple on Fitzwilliam
> kiss and kiss again, the world's rough edges
> briefly smooth as they linger to drift
> and pause along the railings,
> their eyelids closing out the day.

O'Donnell does not advocate surrender; her poems are fiercely committed. If the lovers close their eyes, it is to gather strength for the fight, not to retreat: earlier in the poem, she recalls not emigrating in the last recession, 'believing we were gifted. / The privilege of nation, hoped in, / treated gently by our like, came to us. / There was no other place.' 'The World is Mine' is an important poem in this collection and sounds the key-note: here is a poet at ease, in full possession of her consciousness and thus of the world around her. The poem surveys Ireland and concludes:

> From Antrim to Wexford, sun has spilt
> across the sleeping island, till Galway, Limerick
>
> steady themselves into full colour, as I once
> steadied myself when I was ten and watched
> an orchard brightening, seized my day.

This is an admirable, interesting and varied collection, in a clean, readable production by Arc Publications. We celebrate the presence amongst us of a wise, knowing poet like Mary O'Donnell and the gift of a collection like this one.

Gerry Murphy's *Muse* is a curious book. If Mary O'Donnell is a bard, it is tempting to call Murphy a jester. His poems are often funny (the collection opens with a priceless line: 'I am writing naked / at the kitchen table'), but he is no comedian. Rather, comedy is a device through which he tests his art. *Muse* wishes to examine where poetry comes from, hence the collection's title – whether it is from love, sex, politics, religion, or the various minor incidents of a life: taking a photograph of a couple of British tourists ('Peace Process'), for instance, or the decaying radio signal from Apollo 11 ('A Farewell to Neil Armstrong'). In 'Turn', he imagines a woman (a lover?) walk out of a restaurant to make a phone call. As she turns to come back,

> a rare gleam of sunlight,
> angling through the rooftop louvres,
> snags in your still blonde hair
> and suddenly you're eighteen
> all over again.

The poems here, of course, aspire to the condition of that beam of light, angled in a way to reveal the lasting beauty amidst 'quotidian dullness'.

There are nineteen poems 'after' someone else – Milton, Miłosz, Mahon, Rumi, Neruda, the ninth-century Irish. Murphy's poems are nothing close to imitations; rather, they take the original and make of it something quite new. So, 'Deus Ex Machina' appropriates a phrase from Mahon and we get:

What monstrous intervention
explains this enormous gearbox
rusting in the forest?

Closer to the original is 'A Pact', after Pound: Murphy substitutes Orpheus
for Whitman; he resists Orpheus (rather than 'detests' the father-figure,
as in Pound's poem); he is a grown man with a long childhood, not a
'grown child' with 'pig-headed father', as in Pound; and so on. Murphy
finds inspiration in these other poems and uses them to try to flush out
his own Muse. The presence of ghostly doubles in the more successful
poems towards the end of the collection testifies, it seems, to an interest
in the mysterious source of the poetic gift. In 'Revenant', he encounters a
ghost on the stairs.

Not six feet away,
the ghost of some
previous tenant,
staring at me frankly,
with a hint
of a smile just faded,
or just about to break
on his lips.

This is an energetic, sparkling and witty collection that will enhance
Murphy's already substantial reputation.

Splendid as they are, the difference between the very fine collections
that O'Donnell and Murphy have produced and poetry of the very highest
order lies in the doubt pervading the poems, or, rather, the extent to
which the poet allows him- or herself reside within uncertainty – the
poet's 'Negative Capability', in Keats's famous phrase. In Mahon, Heaney
and Plath, the poem and the thought that gives the poem its momentum
seem to unfurl together; a world invents itself as we read, seemingly
afresh with every reading. This is the case with Sara Berkeley Tolchin's
wonderful book.

That *What Just Happened* is a mature, resonant book is evident from
early on. 'If I Met You Now' very gently leans on a familiar, even clichéd
idea of life as a journey across a storm-tossed sea, allowing the idea to
generate a metaphor that empowers, not overpowers, the poem:

I need to sail alone. Sometimes
I look from shore to shore,
the difference between twenty-eight
and forty-four; my world tips up

and they come pouring out of me,
songs I could never have sung back then.

We learn from the biographical notes that Berkeley Tolchin lives on the
west coast of the United States and that she works as a hospice nurse.
Some of the poems take America's Pacific coast or the care homes she
works in as their landscape. Canada geese appear in a number of poems,
including the exquisite, dense poem, 'Sun and Standing Still'. In 'South
Beach', she visits a beach with her daughter:

> ... we stood together there
> at the ragged edge of the land
> and the churn and rush of the waves merged in a rising choir,
> a melody, not sweet, but urgent, uncontrolled;
>
> it sang of me and her,
> of the earth that arose, bold,
> from the featureless ocean, the hill of the world,
> and of all mothers and their wild unpredictable girls

The lightness of touch in evidence here is visible too in a number of elegies
in the book, some inspired, it seems, by the poet's day job. 'Barn's Burned
Down', for instance, is a stunning elegy for a lost patient. 'Burrow Beach'
is as good a poem as has been published in Ireland in recent years. Another
elegy, this time for Berkeley Tolchin's mother, it is highly accomplished.
'Rage, rage / against the dying of the light', she quotes Dylan Thomas,
then goes on:

> and that is what I am doing each day,
> raging in my own distilled and private way,
>
> nothing showy — it's not what she would want —
> but that doesn't make less bitter or less deep
> the sorrow that breaks over me before I sleep.

The title poem illuminates the collection, as one might expect:

> Miners are trained when things go wrong
> to lie on the ground, breathe slow
> and shallow, wait until the light breaks at last
> through a chink and they are found.
> Sometimes behind their self-made barricades
> they lie there breathing low
> until their lives rise up and float around

above them, no colours they've ever seen,
memories shedding light in the coal-dust gloom,
making room for what's to come.

This bold image might be taken as descriptive of Berkeley Tolchin's
efforts as a poet – a peaceful, oxygen-conserving state allows one's life
to 'rise up and float around' and become visible, coloured, and enables
movement forward. She seems to say this another way in 'Coyotes', the
collection's final poem:

You have to be the architect of your life,
the poet of it, hunger for what the future holds,
face the inevitable, the unknown and, like the coyotes,
pound down the double doors of the night and come out
fires blazing, eyes wide open, heart alight.

This is an excellent description of this book; *What Just Happened* is certainly
a clear-sighted, heart-stirring collection of enormous force.

Jean O'Brien

SUPPOSE

Suppose that the hammer's trajectory
had been a fraction more to the left,
the wind direction easterly instead
of west, or that he had turned his head
instinctively on hearing something
whoosh through the air, it would have been
a different story.

Suppose when I went into mother's room,
excited, to show my latest trawl of tadpoles,
swimming their endless question marks
in the Mason jar, she had turned instead
and dashed them to the floor where they floundered
open mouthed and drowning in air, rather
than distractedly pushing me out
towards the door with a murmur of 'Nice. Nice'.

Suppose I had not turned at the last moment
to see her raise her hand armed with a claw
hammer and heft it through the already cracked
glass pane of the window with a shout:
'Now you'll fix it, you bastard!'

I did, though –

and everything splintered and through
the gaping maw of the frame I saw
my baby brother sit quietly
in the garden, a red blanket under him
glass shards glittering all around like Chinese
luck money and just beyond in the long
grass, the hammer with its head and cleft
buried and rendered harmless.

Suppose my Father and Aunt had seen it
from my vantage point; and not what they thought
they saw, my troubled Mother fling a hammer
at my brother's head, had I not froze, been
too shocked to talk, I could have told them.
The Doctor came and they gentled her out
into the waiting car. She returned weeks later –
eyes shattered, her speech hammered fragments.

Simon Kew

MY BOX OF LIES

It was like I kept them on a shelf in a rusty and unremarkable tin box,
positioning them between a case of old screws and some lino off-cuts.
I quickly learnt to let a nest of mature deceits rest, settle themselves
into the murk with maybe an occasional tweak. Later, I'd contemplate
adding the curled lead of another: *yeah, made it to Frome in two hours.*
A new fiction gathers clammily around the fingers because the hidden
Lloyd's account is itself a snaky item. It takes a dextrous hand to shake
a writhing whopper into a tin of wriggling fibs; lies don't like each other –
black or white. A new one's an especially conscious thing; it sneaks for
wriggle-room, explaining why I was in John Lewis (where Trish works)
and on Thursday and why do I need two mobiles – the second-guessing
what a wife might think, burrowing myself into imagined conversations,
the question which hasn't yet emerged, feeding up the larval lies, cobbling
connections for the ask. And what does a lying hound look like anyway?

Moyra Donaldson

NOT METAPHORS
  – for Claire

I do not accidentally come across them
in misty fields, or in old gateways,
I'm aware of where they are,
day in, day out and though always
astonished by the centuries in their eyes,
the grace and beauty of their being,
I also know how much they piss and shit.
I've wheeled thousands of barrow-loads
of dung to the muck heap.

My horses need fed, groomed, shod.
They strain tendons, cut themselves,
get ulcers, viruses, mud fever
and need the vet; colic during the night.
Are they warm enough, safe enough?
Is that one losing weight,
or this one's sacroiliac flaring up?

My horses are schooled and taught
to carry themselves properly, work
through from behind, maintain a light
contact, meet a jump on the right stride,
bascule to perfection; leave the poles up.
That's a lot of work for me and my horses
and sometimes we make mistakes –
fall and get hurt; actually hurt.

Fiona Sze-Lorrain

WALKING OUT

When men take from me all the heat and light, I content myself
    with echoes, sounds, and radio waves in every room up for sale inside

this body. What's gone stretches each wall so terribly that when
    I cough, mud bricks give up their secrets and poor decisions. One

of the corners keeps the song alive, another too wet for dust
    or sprigs to rot gently. I manage. To obey an inner despot, I check

the doors, sweep the balcony, and reframe each picture with clouds
    or perfect fruits as focus. For inspiration, I look out the windows.

I am inside each window, the window moves in me. Anything you see
    from the outside – the garden, the hare, disposable bin, and wayfaring

tree – teaches you to live with used spaces. Touch pain by its rim:
    under your bed, in the cellar. I am still here because of my dilemma.

In this scenario, a glass of water and a pill are two separate issues.
    Look at you. The solitude. Even the cactus is softening each kill.

Evan Jones

IN THE WORLD

Moya Cannon, *Keats Lives* (Carcanet Press, 2015), €9.99.
Eamon Grennan, *There Now* (The Gallery Press, 2015), €11.95.
Justin Quinn, *Early House* (The Gallery Press, 2015), €11.95.

Moya Cannon's poems are warm and personal. The parent-child relation
is her great theme in *Keats Lives*, which she conceives of and pulls apart
through the variety of little situations in which her speaker finds herself.
In 'I wanted to show my mother the mountains –', landscape becomes an
opportunity to consider her mother's death; in 'Finger-fluting in Moon-
Milk', a trip through the prehistoric caves in Dordogne inspires a consideration of an adult artist showing the act of creation – which is also the
act of defiling nature, the need to leave a mark – to a child:

> a woman, it seems, with a baby on her hip
> trailed her fingers down through
> the soft, white substance
> extruded by limestone cave-walls
> and the child copied her.

Cannon is subtle, and the moment is not exploited beyond that gentle
trailing of fingers. So it's the copying that becomes important, and the
relationship, which is a kind of teaching or mentoring. The title poem,
'Keats Lives on the Amtrak', performs similarly, as the speaker, on a 'silver
train / between Philly and New York', is confronted by a conductor who
wants to know why her novel is 'full of page-markers'. He is, it turns out,
a Keats fan. Here the relationship is more reciprocal as speaker and subject
learn from each other: 'He leaned forward, smiled, and said, / "I'm going to
get a t-shirt with / *Keats Lives* on it."' His fandom, as the poem progresses,
reveals his unexpected depths to the speaker, and makes such an impression that it is the clear occasion for the poem: an exchange of ideas about
the poet Keats in the – why not? – dining car of an American train. But
it's a less subtle poem in its way than 'Finger-fluting', because the occasion
seems to revel in the surprise and perhaps exoticism of finding a conductor
who is a Keats fan. I like better the poems where Cannon's teacher-self
shows more wisdom, like 'Molaise', an ekphrastic poem about the oak
statue of St Molaise, now in the National Museum, which asks questions
about the statue's origins, draws on her knowledge of the Middle Ages, and
concludes, sweetly:

I, now in middle age, am past denying
that I have known women and men
in whose presence I am calmed and blessed,
under whose compassionate gaze I am complete
as the storm-rounded stones on Inishmurray's beach.

Eamon Grennan's *There Now* is a book of painterly poems, the lines long
followed by short, swinging in slow brushstrokes back and forth across the
canvas. There are, to be certain, a couple of Cézanne references, a Bon-
nard, Gauguin, Manet, and, God, Renoir ('whose paintings I don't much
like' – Charles Wright), which puts the visuals into an impressionistic
spectrum of colour and image. There are also plenty of flowers, leaves,
nature morte, on the one hand; but these are juxtaposed against bird and
birdsong on the other. 'With Rainbow and Two Ravens' is typical of the
kind of observations prevalent in the book:

Whatever that rainbow might mean those ravens never mind it
        as they spindrift over High Road houses
calling to each other with such lofty indifference
        for anything that might otherwise distract them

That 'indifference' is the significant word here (it comes up again in a poem
a few pages later, 'Among the Elements in a Time of War' – 'as if the
stricken face of earth itself / with its indifference for a moment broken /
could not stop sobbing'). The birds are indifferent to the plot and plotting of the poet, who brings the birds and natural occurrence together to
create drama. It's a sort of double pun, because that 'plotting' is central
to the birds' indifference. For who else but the poet himself scattered the
crumbs in another poem to attract the birds, so that they are seen 'squabbling for a shiny morsel' ('Crumbs'), or they 'squabble over breadcrumbs'
('Things in the Vicinity'), or they are 'chattering among / scattered
breadcrumbs' ('World Word') or even, again, 'quarrelling among the
crumbs' ('Leaving'). Why is it only crumbs for the birds? They only cause
squabbling – which we might take as metaphor for human relations, the
poet breading the landscape for drama. But if so then why is the poet
revelling in all this? What's innocent, it seems, is in the natural world alone,
and that is what Grennan is seeking. He calls it, in 'World Word', 'the
out-of-sight unspoken never-to-be-known pure / sense-startling untranslatable *there* of the world as we find it'. For we do have to find it, 'out
of nature' as we are. At the same time, there, on which the book's title
hinges, 'remains beyond my ken', Grennan tells us in the same poem. But
in another, 'While', there might be 'the ever-changing light ... up /
again as always to its old unspeakable unstoppable tricks'. The unspeakable,
the untranslatable elements of the world: in *There Now* – one meaning of

which is a kind of reassurance – Grennan observes the natural world and takes comfort in what he cannot find words for.

Meanwhile, in Prague, Justin Quinn is thinking about loss. 'Lost Child', one of two longer poems in *Early House*, follows the poet's train of thought as a neighbourly 'they' call their child home – a child who doesn't answer. While Quinn is himself a kind of lost child, a migrant of Europe, the poem doesn't dwell on that angle openly. It begins by following the action, creating tension in the child's lack of response by imagining his whereabouts (possibly tragic, likely not). From there it expands beyond the initial occasion as the speaker allows himself to become complicit with the outcome:

> ... I am the child
> or panicked father standing in the road.
> I am the neighbour watching from a window
> wondering if I should go down to help.
> Events will turn and make me with their will.

Between the allusive rhymes, there's an anxiety – Larkin's 'then fear' of ageing and loss, of the tragedies life can set before you. But the gravity, what keeps the poet set in his thinking, is where the poem ends, as he enters deeper into the scenario his mind is creating: 'I might become the man who works the land / in common'. That worker of the common land sounds so Heaney-ish, no? So while at one level the poem is a sort of anti-fantasy that pushes the poet to accept multiple futures (like Edward Thomas' ploughman: 'If we could see all all might seem good'), at another the errant poet is considering his place, as the lost child becomes middle-aged. Paralleling this, though not nearly as dramatic, the book opens with 'A Glove', a snappy little number about the lost member of a pair – another metaphor. It ends: 'I lost a glove, / then lost the other. / I'd no more forms / that could withhold / the snows, the storms, / the perishing cold.' And again that perishing loss, the glove a symbol of protection and defence, the inability of the poet to keep the pair together. Poems about loss and the fear of loss pervade *Early House*. Jeff Buckley sets the tone in 'Singer':

> His lovely body and his lovelier voice
> are lost. The world has kept such sweetness longer
> so many times before amidst its noise –
> the real cause must be much worse and much stronger.

Son of musician Tim Buckley, who died of an overdose in 1975, the young Buckley drowned in the Mississippi River in 1994, fully clothed, an 'accidental death' by accounts. Here, the anxiety and the drawing of connections between art and death foreshadow the major poem in the book. 'Letter, Including Bears', addressed to the Berlin-based British poet Alistair Noon, a fine rhymester in his own right, is a *tour de force*, a poem I could read more of, taking in a moment of life and history (always treacherous when those two intertwine) in Central Europe. Think Putin, soldiers, Crimea. The speaker is drinking away in a Czech pub, its yard packed with 'tanks and armoured cars parked in a line / for kids to clamber on, a rusted rearguard / the Russians left behind in '89'. 'I like to sit here and consider things', Quinn tells us, 'While this inflated bear, the brewery's logo, / considers me. Irish. Letter writer. / ... Basically, driftwood.' The self-admissions, the casualness, mixed with the anxiety about the world at large underlay the epistolary poem, which is again about a man wondering about his place in the world, and how that place might change very soon – and very easily – for the worse.

Kate Noakes

BEFORE I CAN WALK AGAIN

I do not remember how many
pairs of boots are in the wardrobe
or how many need re-heeling
or the number of summer dresses I own
that actually fit, or before you no longer
wanted to, the number of nights
you slept in my bed.

I don't recall the number of hours
I can stare out of the window
at pigeons and crows, or the weeks
the Pantheon's been scaffolded
and sheeted, or how many nights
I've listened to music to herald sleep
or how many I've not.

I don't remember the number
of socks and earrings
I've lost, or necklaces I've broken
or how long the nights
I've slept alone
or, how long those nights
I will sleep, alone.

John McKernan

I LIKE TO WALK MILES IN OMAHA

Down to the Missouri River
When it is below zero outside

And say my name
To the ice the snow
The black clouds

It helps me to remember
When I was small
Inside my mother's womb
Her red blood cells

And the future
Corn
Wheat
Soybeans
My tiny warm body How it would grow

Jacqueline Thompson

HOUSEKEEPER

I put eyes and tongues into every
dumb object I encounter, finding
smiles in fire-grates, laughter
tinkling in the servants' bell.

I console the long silver spoon
as I polish her and all her daughters.
I stroke the cheeks of dusty clocks,
wipe sweat from leaky windows.

As I scrape up luncheon crumbs
he grumbles again: his women left him
out of spite. Tears mottle skin as dry
as moths entombed in wardrobes.

My cuckoo master laid his eggs
in umpteen nests: wife,
stepdaughter, chambermaid;
but never prune-fleshed me.

I used to hear his grunts then watch
them scuttle from his room. Now
I cannot shake the cat-in-the-wall
ache bricked-up in my chest.

I have stayed here too long.
I am as dried out and stuck
as rice abandoned in a pot.
I'll never leave.

Mary Montague

APPARITION

Alcedo atthis

A different kind of grotto
where a supplicant willow
strokes the canal's still waters.
There. The shimmer of an answer
as the bird alights: mantle
of heaven; breast of earth; spear
of bill; throat of white.

It perches like a bunsen-flame,
drawing canal bank pilgrims
who linger to whisper
praise. They gasp
when the fisher of minnows
plunges – a blue dart
that knifes the gaze.

Zoë Brigley Thompson

RAVISHMENT

> (noun) 1. rapture or ecstasy; 2. violent removal; 3. the forcible
> abduction of a woman; 4. rape.

If she is a well, stony in solitude,
the one who loves her is a seeker
lowered down on a rope in the dark
to rescue whatever creature
or child, clutching an arm
or a leg, might lie at bottom.

       ★   ★   ★

I have written to you so many times
about closed courtyards, the spring
that wells up in Song of Solomon,
the rose garden that my grandfather
tended, where the gorgeous faces
of flowers gazed at the smouldering
wreckage of cars. Only you know
that the interior place I dreamed
was a garden razed, the door split
on its hinges and gaping, and how
to shore up that small square space
enough to unfasten myself for you?

Gerard Smyth

LEVELS OF CONVERSATION

Rita Ann Higgins, *Tongulish* (Bloodaxe Books, 2016), £9.95.
Martina Evans, *The Windows of Graceland* (Carcanet Press, 2016), £12.99.
Cathal McCabe, *Outer Space* (Metre Editions, 2016), €12.

While there is no discernible note suggesting these three poets are kindred spirits, two of them, Rita Ann Higgins and Martina Evans, do share a style that tends to be conversational, and both display particular skills with the narrative form to great effect (Higgins' 'The Mission' might well be her finest poem; in Evans' case, family and local characters from her Cork background are essential to the momentum of her storylines).

While heat and energy come off the pages of *Tongulish* and *The Windows of Graceland*, Cathal McCabe, in his first full collection, delivers a cooler, more restrained note, often in a more formal style. *Outer Space* is abundant in its inventiveness and in the changes of structure as well as the different shades and textures from poem to poem.

Higgins has always been a poet with a distinctive stance, never shirking her responsibilities as a public voice speaking on behalf of those who do not possess such a platform. When she states that 'Galway seagulls' are 'unfussy, / they go straight for the jugular' ('Shades of Truth'), she might well be referring to herself. 'Unfussy' is one of her characteristics. She is also both jocular and jugular, two traits that combine to make her a singular voice in Irish poetry. She has long been a tough-minded, waspish critic of the establishment, calling to mind the satiric tongue-lashings of Austin Clarke, a poet whose authoritative voice was one of the few in his day to point out the failures, smugness and hypocrisies of the new State he had witnessed coming into existence.

Her poems, like Clarke's castigating satires (he was our best satirist since Swift), have an authority that is lacking in the work of others who see themselves as the new troubadours of protest and dissent, and whose combative views are often (as the critic Adam Kirsch once said of Yvor Winters) 'promulgated like papal bulls'.

The social and political commentary in Higgins' work might be jocular in tone and language but this never overshadows the gravity of her sympathies and compassion. ('The Carer' is a thoughtful example of this – a poem that gets under the skin of the heartbreak and frustration of that vocation). This, along with other poems in *Tongulish*, shows the flipside of Higgins' jocular mood: its gravity and sombre truth-telling. While she can be 'entertaining', nothing is packaged for easy consumption. Any impression of spontaneity in her 'conversational tone' is misleading; she is very precise in the words she chooses.

'The Women of 1916' is another of the engaging poems here – honouring, as it does, another corps of the banished and forgotten: those women who, until fairly recently, were airbrushed from history. Higgins tackles emotive subjects ('Mr Grave Offence') but does so in a way deliberately managed to keep the language from straying into rhetoric. When she lets her ire rip ('The Gathering'), her ingrained humour becomes the enabling force of the poem. This is demonstrated again in the fun that she knocks out of ancient Rome in a number of the poems ('Caligula', 'My Claudius', 'Sinner'). Passion and conviction walk hand-in-hand in these poems.

The cover image on Martina Evans' *The Windows of Graceland*, a broken guitar with a picture postcard of the Lakes of Killarney inset into the larger image, suggests that we may be entering the country of folksiness. This, however, is folksiness with an edge: Evans might not be a lakeside romantic but she is a romantic, a poet of the Costcutter's and Sainsbury's generation, preoccupied with the more mundane joys and fears – and even admitting her shoe addiction ('The Mystery of Shoes'). She takes the risk of placing herself centre stage in much of her work – but this is part of its vitality, and necessary to the anecdotal nature of many of her poems. She has done what most good poets do: invented a style to accommodate her often quirky world (a talking cat, a Chinese puppeteer, a Munster dentist who 'played the drill like Hendrix').

Evans staked out her real poetic terrain – and has maintained an imaginative foothold there – in the Cork homeplace of her childhood and youth, and has made that place, Burnfort, as familiar to us as Heaney's Derry or Kavanagh's Monaghan. She is terrific at excavating her rich store of memory and her local watchfulness enriches her best poems, memorialising place and family – particularly a mother-daughter relationship of which she makes full and fruitful use, and which yields the haunting 'Goodnight Irene'.

The subject matter and this preoccupation with a personal past might be nostalgic, but Evans is never in the mood for gentle reminiscence. Her Cork inheritance is not only familial but cultural and political as well, providing a wide frame of references. These extend far beyond any form of provincialism. Her scenes from Burnfoot reflect universal experiences. She moves with ease between that rural Ireland of the past and metropolitan London: Balls Pond Road is now legibly on the poetry map.

If Kavanagh was creatively refreshed through his relationship with Dublin, so too is Evans in her London settings – there are several very fine poems evoking that sense of dislocation: 'London Irish', 'On the Border', 'The Dawning of the Day'. The centuries-old complexities of Anglo-Irish relations are ingeniously rendered, and condensed, in another poem, 'Two Hostages'. And, of course, there are the places to which the imagination makes its pilgrimages – in Evans' case, Graceland and her Arcadian 'Burnfort, Las Vegas'. While her 'nostalgia for her Catholic childhood' might be complex, as the book's blurb suggests, her nostalgia for a bygone heyday is simple enough:

> We move the Sacred Heart lamp
> closer to Elvis's face now in the month
> of June.

If sometimes there appears to be an element of exaggeration in Evans' retrospection, it has an appealing quality. Politics is local and in the past: the IRA war of independence, Black and Tan reprisals, the burning of Mallow. Her nod towards 1916 comes in an incantatory two-stanza poem on the fiftieth anniversary in which every line of the first stanza is repeated in reverse in the second stanza – an imaginative device suggesting, perhaps, that commemoration locks us in a kind of stasis.

But then a poem such as 'Omar Khadr' reminds us, shatteringly, of the moment we live in now. The cumulative effect of this *Selected* is to suggest that Evans is a true original with a voice that is unmistakable – and despite the zaniness and chattiness of much of her work, a very serious poet.

Like Evans, many of Cathal McCabe's best poems dwell in a private and familial world, and it is here that he is most fluent and in command ('A Rose Given to My Mother', 'Meeting in Outer Space', and the exquisite 'Elegy for Molly McCabe').

His quick intelligence is matched by the formidable rigour of his approach – a rigour which never makes his poems unapproachable. He proceeds from line to line with exactitude of utterance, delivering refined and crystalline phrases. A striking feature are the shifts, his willingness to try different routes on the expanded map of poetry: 'Night Club', among a few others here, suggests a poet with a 'Beat' sensibility, the quick pared-down riff; elsewhere, as in 'Summer in Killowen', he can summon a vivid lyric moment reminiscent of Mahon:

> The trees' manic
> midnight shadows
> flailing a bedroom wall.
>
> Why ever panic?
> A father knows
> they're shaking free the day's lost ball.

In fact, Mahon seems a dominant influence as well as being the subject of a homage. Echoes of Beckett too – not only in the existential anxieties but in the clipped, summarising language, as in 'The Mountains of Mourne':

> here the urn
> here the remains
> here we mourn
> here we weep
> down
> to the sea

His presence in his own poems is low-key compared to Higgins and Evans, and I suspect his more detached outlook has been formed under the influence of European and, especially, Polish poetry. In fact it seems McCabe's sense of how his work should sound and look has been shaped through his affinities with the poetry of Eastern Europe as much as from what he has absorbed from the more lyrically opulent Irish climate. His poem 'The Stone' (for Zbigniew Herbert) is an example of how this marriage of influences puts a different finish on his work.

While intensity seems to be a chief characteristic, he can move from the tenderness of 'Love Poem' (among other beautiful allusions to his children) to the emotional moments of elegy ('To My Mother'). A poem of fond remembrance such as 'Homage to Mortons' is a refreshing take on the 'memorialising poem', in how it rediscovers and captures the particulars of a time and place.

I found the interludes of typographical playfulness ('The Roof', 'Night in Jastarnia', 'We're Off to the Zoo, We'll Be Back By Noon') an irritating distraction from a poet who is otherwise sure-footed with his variations. These poems do nothing to strengthen the overall architecture of this fine collection.

Amanda Bell

COMPLICIT

When my stolen gun
was unearthed,
tarp-wrapped,

my hands recalled
the satin of its patinated
stock, the greasy feel

of the canvas bag
I used to carry shells;
soft drift of down

from felled wild fowl,
which rolled up into rags
at my cold touch.

I wonder, in the weft of prints,
what links my hands
to shallow graves –

but this is titillating guilt,
which doesn't implicate
my green-washed life

in drowned Pacific islands,
with each switch I flick,
each spark of my ignition.

John Murphy

LOTUS

No one knows you. And you know no one.
Not even your children. But life and history
are lived one day at a time, and rather than lie alone
on your bed with an unlit cigarette, go to your children,
tell them a story, someone else's, or one
that comes to you like a long forgotten song
your mother sang, days before you were born.
Speak, read a few pages, learn to listen
for the sound of children listening, and soon
it will be too dark to read and you will go alone
into a trust you have been given with words
that are more than spaced silences.
No one knows you, but if they listen to you,
tell them a story. It doesn't matter if it's true.

David Romanda

DEATHBED POEM

I wish
This mattress
Wasn't so
Bloody comfy

David Clink

A PREMONITION OF RAIN

The skies empty.

On these days our umbrellas talk
to each other in whispers.

They wait weeks for these days.

You can hear them.
You bend in to listen.

The sky is falling –
that is what they are saying.

But you look on the bright side,
take a sick day, watch movies, make popcorn.

Just outside the window, the world –
pine cones, pavement, cars.

The constant threat of sun.

Jo Gill

WAYS OF REMEMBERING

Lucy Collins, *Contemporary Irish Women Poets* (Liverpool University Press, 2015), hb £75.

The first thing to say about this new study is that it offers a useful reminder of just how much scholarship is out there on the work of modern and contemporary Irish women poets. Lucy Collins is to be credited for having surveyed and, where appropriate, synthesized this material even if, in so doing, she risks leaving herself with only a relatively small patch of yet-to-be-explored territory. Her chosen focus is on memory and on the many and various ways in which her selected poets remember and represent the past – their own, their nation's, their generation's, their gender's. At each stage, Collins has necessarily to qualify, redefine and nuance her terms. The result, in its best moments, is an argument that is subtle and perspicacious. On occasion, though, the terms become so slippery, so tentative, that the meaning slips out of sight and I sometimes – especially in the Introduction and opening 'Concepts' section – wished for a clearer steer as to the argument and its implications. Evidently, though, it is the process (or more properly, 'processes') of remembering that are Collins' and her poetic subjects' primary interest. This is a valuable line to take because it enables the author to bring a number of different ways of remembering into scope, to look at continuity and change across time, and to trace the challenges for these poets of engaging with their task.

Within this broad arc, Collins assesses poetic memory in relation to place, history, tradition, the body and 'poetic practice'. The sense of place is excellent, and I particularly liked the attentiveness throughout the book to different locations both within and beyond Ireland, and the refusal to homogenize national identity. I found the notion of history to be rather static, though. 'Historiography' might have been a more useful term than 'history' in articulating this shaping of memory and its representation – in other words, not simply what happened, but the processes by which we select, capture and relate what (we think) happened.

The treatment of 'poetic practice' is, similarly, a little insecure. The introduction asserts a continuity between these poets' work and that of their antecedents but thereafter, with one or two exceptions such as the brief but excellent account of Catherine Walsh's engagement with Language poetry, and a belated nod to some precursors in the conclusion, there is surprisingly little reference to these poets' relationship with their peers or their familiarity with wider trends in literary culture. That a number of them (Eavan Boland, for example) began to explore the potential of life-writing in the 1980s and 1990s at precisely the moment when the field – partly as a consequence of new feminist scholarship – was undergoing something of a critical renaissance tells us as much about their engagement with this larger body of work as it does about the intricacies of their personal pasts. Likewise, and in the same period, the turn to fairy tales as a metaphor for women's experience might be read not only as a figure for the poet's own memories, but as a response to, or conversation with, the work of other contemporary writers – Anne Sexton and Angela Carter, to name just two. My point here is that features identified as characteristic of these poets' exploration of memory and its relation to national identity become available to them, at least in part, because the broader literary culture offers these motifs. In this respect, the poets are more connected, more engaged, than the narrative otherwise seems to imply and the memories to which they refer are not always or necessarily theirs alone. Collins describes women as a 'marginalized' group but I am not persuaded, on the evidence of the poetry, that these female poets are quite so marginalized from broader cultural trends and textual practices. All this having been said, there are some fine discussions here of the work of individual poets. Collins is admirably attentive to changes (or conversely, continuities) in her poets' work over time and the book offers a valuable account both of the breadth and depth of contemporary poetry by women in Ireland.

In the first 'Concepts' section, the discussion of Boland provides an insightful reading of the significance of the poet's relatively privileged London childhood. Collins' exploration of repetition, or 'relentless reinforcement', is of particular note. Also in this section, Chapter Two, 'Between Here and There: Migrant Identities and the Contemporary Irish Woman Poet' goes some way to mapping a global context with reference to Sinéad Morrissey in Japan and Eva Bourke in her native Germany. Chapter Three, 'Private Memory and the Construction of Subjectivity', considers the difficult associations that attach to the use of the lyric, and the lyric 'I', with reference to Mary O'Malley, Paula Meehan and, more recently, Colette Bryce. The reading of the formal properties of the poetry is insightful and suggestive.

In the second part of the book, 'Achievements', individual poets including Eiléan Ní Chuilleanáin, Medbh McGuckian, Catherine Walsh and Vona Groarke, get a chapter each. It's a good tactic, allowing Collins to pick up and develop some of the ideas that were flagged up in a more abstract way in the first part. The role of silence – the refusal or inability to remember and to express, or 'the silence of the past' – in Ní Chuilleanáin's poetry, and its deep self-reflexivity, are considered with sensitivity and tact, as is the important point of difference between Ní Chuilleanáin and Boland with respect to the question of history. The significance of architecture in the work of the former is also usefully addressed, establishing a line that is picked up in the later discussion of Walsh and Groarke. In the case of McGuckian, the alienating and unreliable properties of language are the initial focus, taking us – inevitably, perhaps – to a discussion of pure abstraction, as embodied by the sacred figure of the angel. Collins rightly points to the influence of 'medieval and Renaissance art' on the evolution of this figure, but there are other important palimpsests from William Blake through to Wallace Stevens, Allen Ginsberg and Sexton, that have a bearing on McGuckian's use of this figure and our reading of it. Walsh's experimentation (and contemporary criticism's reluctance or inability to fully engage with work in this vein) occupy the next chapter. It's good to see a discussion of Walsh's representation of the suburbs here, indicating that this is a significant space to other poets besides Boland.

The final chapter, on Vona Groarke, rather provocatively questions the premise of the whole collection in its discussion of Groarke's rejection of the label 'Irish poet' and of the idea that there is a 'single cultural location as a central enquiry of the poetry'. As Collins, reading Groarke, shows, the position of the 'transnational subject' is arguably of more interest and value to the debate. What's noteworthy here is that even in the most contemporary of contemporary poetry, and even in a context where – as the rest of Collins' book has persuasively argued – stable concepts of history, memory, tradition, place and subjectivity are up for grabs, certain things persist. Here, in Groarke's writing, it is metaphor that continues to do its work, to make connections, to register the association between past and present, subject and reader, memory and poem.

Sean O'Brien

HAMMERSMITH CANTO V

Beneath the East River, there lie in wait
Tunnels, ladders, hatches and the friend
Whose legs were amputated by a train.

You told me once you were deported,
But never how these elements combine.
So long now among the anecdotes, like you

I find the facts are neither here nor there –
The child in love with maps and lithographs
Finds everywhere a match for appetite:

But though it's infinite beneath the lamp,
As memory the world sails out of sight –
And nor am I, if I can see the worklights,

Scaffolding knee-deep in water, the *mise en abîme*
Where girders sweat, and any second now
A disaster site or the scene of a crime you may

Only just have departed. Or dreamed, like me,
The second son you thought you'd never have,
To whom you lent the name you gave the first.

There is a darkness in your mind that means
You cannot read a novel for yourself
And dare not care for music. It's as though

You came into the world with barely half a kit,
Or else are one who lost a life elsewhere
And cannot make it right again. I see you

Moving down the tunnel like a ghost
Who cannot find his level of damnation.
– Then nothing, and the friend is never named

And you can never quite be placed, although
You surface briefly in Southampton
Like a rumour spread by rumour,

As if you were a story, with a plot
Or even understanding to impart.
Lately I've been watching *Ocean Terminal*

Where the great Cunarders vanish in the fog
And the Scummers broke the strike, the story goes –
Though history says otherwise –

And a page of Baudelaire appears
On a desk in a shipping office, magnified
By oceanic lenses, words themselves

Alone, transported from the world alone,
And now, among the long-dead reefs of paper
In this room that turns to nowhere, I can read

A version of that language still,
Inert with promise, as at last, for all
The lies and geography, we proved to be.

The child in love with maps and lithographs
Finds everywhere a match for appetite:
But though it's infinite beneath the lamp,
As memory the world sails out of sight.

One morning we embark. The mind ablaze,
The heart blown up with rancour and disease,
We set out with the rhythm of the tide,
Infinitude adrift on finite seas.

Some do it to escape the hated State;
Some flee the horrors of indoors, and some –
Stargazers blinded by a woman's stare –
Outrun the lure of Circean perfume,

And rather than be beasts consign themselves
To space and light and skies of molten brass,
Where biting cold and heat that roasts them black
Will slowly mask the imprint of her kiss.

But the authentic travellers are those
Who, light as balloons, take off and never give
Consideration to the claims of fate
And, never asking why, demand to live.

Such men's desires map themselves in clouds.
They dream the way a squaddie dreams a gun,
Of unknown pleasures, protean and vast,
Out where the writ of language cannot run.

Anthony Caleshu

I AM NOURISHING THE POLAR STAR AGAIN

I am nourishing the polar star again and because
I am nourishing the polar star, it is bigger
and brighter than even this streetlight
under which we are standing. The light cast
is paler than our shadows. Though this could be
an allegory, it would be a poor allegory,
unless you consider allegories for their distinction.
In order to distinguish our shadows from the street
– so grey, so tired – a passing policeman
chalks our outline … which, if I may be so anti-
authority, bears me so little resemblance –
the size of my head, the size of my heart –
      'Heart?' my lover interrupts.
      'Heart,' I say.
We go our separate ways, forgetting that
it was under a polar star that we once performed
magnificent tricks of light upon each other.

Peter Sirr

ANYHOW HOW ARE THINGS?

Edited by Jonathan Ellis, *Letter Writing Among Poets from William Wordsworth to Elizabeth Bishop* (Edinburgh University Press, 2015), hb £70.

Who now writes letters? What will survive of us, as far as our correspondence goes, is hasty bits and bytes no sooner sent than forgotten. When it comes to writers, the graduate students of the very near future will be clamouring for access to status updates, likes, retweets, and all the other forlorn ephemera – assuming, of course, that any of it survives.

Yet the power of the letter still compels, and the passion of poets' letters still has the power to move us. As I write this the acclaimed German film *Die Geträumten* (The Dreamed Ones) is about to open – it consists entirely of its two young actors reading the letters of Paul Celan and Ingeborg Bachmann. And if the current century is relatively impoverished, the last was a memorable era in the history of the art of correspondence. Think of Edward Thomas, Marianne Moore, Robert Lowell and Elizabeth Bishop, or Ted Hughes or Philip Larkin, or Robert Duncan and Denise Levertov. And farther back we can turn to Coleridge, Wordsworth, Keats, Shelley, whose letters deepen our sense of their ambitions and achievement and provide in themselves a poetry by other means.

Poets, of all writers, have always been attracted to the letter as a thinking space of its own, a place for self-communion, the articulation of aesthetic positions, a testing ground for ideas, an instrument of the vital companionship by which poetry lives. And poetry itself is, often, an intimate address, pitched for an ideal reader somewhere between the poet's self and the invisible ear of the world. It's not surprising that ever since Ovid and Horace – 'Just as I've told you over and over, Vinny, / Deliver these books of mine to Augustus only / If you know for sure that he's in good health and only / If you know for sure that he's in a good mood ...' ('To Vinius Asina', translation by David Ferry) – poets themselves have been drawn in their own work to the form of the letter. Remember,

> Anyhow how are things?
> Are you still somewhere
> With your long legs
> And twitching smile under
> Your blue hat walking
> Across a place? Or am
> I greedy to make you up
> Again out of memory?
>
> — WS GRAHAM, 'DEAR BRYAN WYNTER'

Or think of Pope, Pound, Auden, MacNeice, Lorine Niedecker, James Schuyler, Derek Mahon, Richard Hugo, Elizabeth Bishop, Ted Hughes, Pablo Neruda, Emily Dickinson, all of whom provide copious examples of what Hugh Haughton in his essay on corresponding poets calls the 'porous borderlines between poems and letters'. Letters veer into poems and poems into letters; the attentive poet will merge both sets of energies. Elizabeth Bishop's 'Letter to N.Y.' for all its formal aplomb sounds exactly like one of her letters; it was one of her great gifts, Haughton reminds us, 'to mimic within her poetry the intimate, joking, conversational tone of the letters'. She even had plans to devote a series of seminars in Harvard on letters.

Letters, of course, may also be the vehicles in which poems are smuggled, especially in the case of poets, like Emily Dickinson, unpublished in their own lifetimes. Both poem and letter, in cases like this, will share the same single, identifiable reader, and maybe the poem might contain the faint hope that it might reach other eyes and ears. The fate of letters is, though, complex. Who is the owner – the writer or the recipient? What is to be done with them after the writer has died? Will they always present the writer in a good light or might they be the subject of scandal? Think of the outrage caused by Larkin's letters and the damage it did to his reputation among the righteous. Many poets or literary estates sought the destruction of their letters. Then again, in other cases, the published correspondence of poets altered and enhanced our view of them and formed an additional corpus of work – Robert Browning and Elizabeth Barrett Browning, or Rossetti's *Letters to his Family*. Maybe the most recent distinguished example of this is the extensive correspondence between Robert Lowell and Elizabeth Bishop, of which Paul Muldoon gives a lively account here.

Hugh Haughton's essay on corresponding poets, one of the most valuable contributions in the book, reminds us of the special weight of poets' letters. He quotes Richard Howard's observation – writing of Marianne Moore – that 'a poet's letters constitute a crucial dimension of the poet'. To read poets' letters to other poets is to gain insight into the context in which they operated and into the complex bond of common obsession and lonely practice that ties and at the same time separates them. It also, of course, casts light on the work itself.

Paul Muldoon's interest in his contribution is specifically in the 'extent to which letters may provide a system for allowing us to better understand a work of art'. A fascinating example of this is the series of letters between Lowell and Bishop in relation to his 'Skunk Hour' and her 'The Armadillo'.

> ... I have six poems started. They beat the big drum too much. There's one in a small voice that's fairly charmingly written I hope (called 'Skunk Hour', not in your style yet indebted a little to your 'Armadillo.')

There's a nice moment when Muldoon catches the inevitable rivalry that underlies a good deal of poets' correspondence. Lowell writes to Bishop to tell her how much he liked her '*New Yorker* fish poem' and confesses that he 'felt very envious in reading it'. Another letter confesses that the debt was greater than he first acknowledged: 'I used your "Armadillo" in class as a parallel to my "Skunks" and ended up feeling a petty plagiarist'. Bishop also famously objected to Lowell's use of private letters from Elizabeth Hardwicke in *The Dolphin*, as in this passage quoted by Muldoon:

> One can use one's life as material ... but these letters – aren't you violat-
> ing a trust? IF you were given permission – IF you hadn't changed them
> ... etc. But *art just isn't worth that much.*

Bishop and Lowell sustained their correspondence, from just after they first met a dinner party in 1947 right up until his death thirty years later, and it was a working correspondence in the sense that both poets sent and reviewed each other's work, set out their artistic stalls, and were each other's most intense readers. Their dependence on each other's response is made clear in *Words in Air: The Complete Correspondence Between Elizabeth Bishop and Robert Lowell*, and that book's co-editor, Thomas Travisano, provides a useful background here to the editing of that continuous river of letters.

Sometimes isolation is the spur to letter writing. In 'Lorine Niedecker's Republic of Letters', Siobhan Phillips deals with one of twentieth-century poetry's most marginalized figures. 'Letters provided what collegiality she could find', and her exchange with Louis Zukovsky, who championed her work and may have fathered her child, was a vital lifeline for her, even if his 'epistolary company could be as difficult as it was sustaining'. Phillips makes the important point that for poets far out of sight of the governing critical consensus, the sense of a smaller, more intimate and accepting audience is key to the poet's selfhood, and the borders between letter and poem are particularly likely to be blurred. She quotes 'Audubon', in which the artist, having failed to find buyers, has turned to his wife:

> must I migrate back
> to the woods unknown, strange
> to all but the birds
> I paint?
>
> Dear Lucy, the servants here
> move quiet
> as killdeer.

Probably the greatest of all the poet letter writers was Keats, whose final letters are treated by Jonathan Ellis in 'Last Letters: Keats, Bishop and Hughes'. In general, useful as some of this volume is as an introduction to the subject, there's no substitute for the real thing:

I am certain of nothing but of the holiness of the Heart's affections and the truth of Imagination—What the imagination seizes as Beauty must be truth—whether it existed before or not—for I have the same Idea of all our Passions as of Love they are all in their sublime, creative of essential Beauty.

— KEATS, LETTER TO BENJAMIN BAILEY, 22 NOVEMBER 1817

We hate poetry that has a palpable design upon us—and if we do not agree, seems to put its hand in its breeches pocket. Poetry should be great & unobtrusive, a thing which enters into one's soul, and does not startle it or amaze it with itself but with its subject.

— KEATS, LETTER TO JH REYNOLDS, 3 FEBRUARY 1818

I think Poetry should surprise by a fine excess and not by Singularity—it should strike the Reader as a wording of his own highest thoughts, and appear almost a Remembrance—2nd Its touches of Beauty should never be half way therby making the reader breathless instead of content: the rise, the progress, the setting of imagery should like the Sun come natural natural too him—shine over him and set soberly although in magnificence leaving him in the Luxury of twilight—but it is easier to think what Poetry should be than to write it—and this leads me on to another axiom. That if Poetry comes not as naturally as the Leaves to a tree it had better not come at all.

— KEATS, LETTER TO JOHN TAYLOR, 27 FEBRUARY 1818

Gerry Cambridge

CROSSING THE FOOTBRIDGE OVER THE CLYDE AT DUSK

The baffle-roar of the spate over the weir down in the valley
behind me, magnifies the silence of those high magenta clouds
tinied by distance on the skyline
with the otherworldly gleam in them at evening.

Far whoops of teenagers, small and particular, off
in the twilight at Blantyre. Wide-skied, dewy chill of autumn.
A first planet, white.
                    Our life together is over.

Paul Muldoon

WALNUTS

1

Bringing to mind the hemispheres of the brain in the brainpan,
these walnut halves are as ripe
for pickling now as in 860, the dye in a Viking girl's under-dress
then being derived from walnut husks. I hear you stifle
a yawn when I note that steamed
black walnut is generally held to be inferior to kiln-dried
while the term *à la mode de Caen*
refers specifically to the braising of tripe
in apple cider. I who have been at the mercy of the cider-press
have also been known to trifle
with the affections of a dryad in a sacred grove,
a judge's daughter and a between-maid to Lord Mountbatten
among others from beyond my clan.
It was only as recently as 1824 we first used the term 'to snipe'.
Walnut was the go-to stock wood for both Brown Bess
and the Lee-Enfield bolt-action, magazine-fed, repeating rifle.
Each has seen service on the shores of Lough Erne
in the hands of both wood-kernes and followers of the First Earl.

2

Our own interpersonal relationships have tended to be so askew
it was only as recently as 1844 we first used the term 'scarf'
of the neck-garter. Girding up the loins
for a family feud has often proved a more fecund
line of inquiry. Walnuts are now deemed
good against malignancies of breast and prostate – not only tried
but tried and true. From time to time you
and I have met on a windswept airfield or wharf
where we've seen fit to join
battle without ever having reckoned
on how the Irish law on treasure trove
would change in the light of the Derrynaflan paten
never mind King Sitric being the son-in-law of King Brian Boru
who prevailed over him at Clontarf
or, at the Boyne,
William of Orange's putting paid to his father-in-law, James II.
It was at the Boyne, you recall, that Ahern
gave Paisley the 'peace bowl' turned from a local walnut-burl.

AN INTERVIEW WITH PAUL MULDOON

> The following interview, which took place on Saturday 23 May
> 2015 at the University of York, was conducted by Alex Alonso and
> Stephen Grace.

SG: Let's begin with your poem 'Cuthbert and the Otters', an elegy for
Seamus Heaney, and the opening poem in your recent collection *One
Thousand Things Worth Knowing* (Faber and Faber, 2015). I'm interested in
how the poem catalogues *stuff* – how it accumulates information, build-
ing by accretion. What, if anything, is being built here?

PM: To be honest, I don't know what it's doing. Somebody said to me
this morning, referring a couple of books back, that there were a lot
of elegies in it. I think what they were saying is, really, there's no need
for that. And I said, well, you know, a lot of people died. I suppose one
shouldn't feel obliged to write something when someone dies, but on the
other hand, I don't think I really did feel obliged in any of the cases where
I've written elegies. They have had to be done, somehow. I certainly
didn't set out to write a poem about Seamus Heaney.

SG: The poem was commissioned initially by the Durham Literature
Festival.

PM: Well, *a* poem was commissioned. As I started out, it was about St
Cuthbert, who's from that part of the world. And as I embarked upon it
then, somehow Seamus … You know, I don't remember the sequence
of it – it wasn't written in sequence. An earlier version was published
at about the time of the literature festival up there. I think Seamus was
mentioned in it, but it was very far removed from the poem that it is
now. But then over the next while, I wrote *that* poem [as it appears in
One Thousand Things Worth Knowing], so that's not the poem that
appeared as the answer to the commission. But one grew into the other.

I suppose, when I've thought about it, it's almost as though one is putting
a lot of stuff out there between one and the world, between one and
the fact. I'm sure it's a protective thing. It's almost as though the poem
is generating this mass of stuff, this blather, and then every so often
goes back to this bald statement: 'I cannot thole the thought of Seamus
Heaney dead.' Really the poem could just be that line, and the rest of the
poem a denial of that fact. That may be a way of thinking about it.

SG: I'm struck by the use of the word 'thole', which seems of a piece with other unfamiliar, arcane items in the poem, but is also at the centre of its emotional charge. How did that word come to you?

PM: It's a word that Seamus identified as a particular usage. He associated it with his childhood and he uses it in his translation of *Beowulf*, as though he were finding a connection with the language of Northern Ireland. It is an Anglo-Saxon usage – I think that's right – but it's related to the word *tollere* or toll, to carry, to endure, so it has cognates in Latin. But it's there because it has a very particular meaning in Seamus Heaney's history.

AA: The new collection is also preoccupied by surveillance, and the conflict between public and private interests. Surveillance is deeply intrusive in 'Rita Duffy: *Watchtower II*', for instance, a poem which looks back to the 'Troubles' and British forces garrisoned on the Irish border. Have you been following developments in the mass surveillance conducted home and abroad by the NSA? And do you sense any overlap between the situation now and the situation in Northern Ireland you address in the poem?

PM: Well let's just remind ourselves of something there: the person who speaks that poem is not actually me, in fact – it's a throwing of the voice, as it were. This person who speaks the poem presents himself and a particular world-picture in which there certainly was a lot of surveillance. There was a point where Northern Ireland was, I'd imagine, of all places in the western world the area where there was most surveillance. Obviously one recoils from the idea of being watched – it makes us uncomfortable even if we're not doing anything wrong.

But one can see the argument for the mass surveillance that operates nowadays. During the London riots [in 2011], for example, where there was a huge amount of looting, many of those involved were caught within about 24 hours because they were either captured on camera or made traceable through their use of mobile phones. I happened to be in the Old Bailey a couple of years ago – just sitting in, I should add – when there was a court case taking place in which a key piece of evidence had to do with mobile phone records. Or consider the mass surveillance taking place at the Boston marathon [in 2013] – it's inappropriate in some sense, but on the other hand we were able to find almost immediately who carried out the terrorist attack. It's a complex issue because one certainly understands the argument that if you're not up to some kind of illegal pursuit, why would you be worried? But of course, it's not exactly as simple as that. I think we do have some rights to privacy.

SG: Do you think people's understanding of what constitutes privacy has changed?

PM: I'm sure that's the case. I'm sure what people reveal about themselves on Instagram and Twitter and Facebook has been a contributing factor towards the adjustment of what privacy means. But if you were living in 1950s Ireland with the priest, the postmistress, and the doctor – not to mention your neighbours – do you seriously think that they didn't know everything about you? If you were living in a mead hall in tenth-century London, say, don't you think everybody knew more about you than you knew about yourself? Did you have privacy then? Were you even an individual then?

I don't think it's a matter of thinking the government is listening to my phone calls, because of course they're not; it seems terribly self-regarding to imagine that they would be. What is troubling though is the extent to which … A couple of years ago I found myself on the internet looking up something to do with archery – one of my abiding interests – and thereafter I started getting e-mails and pop-up notifications about where to buy a bow.

But it's not without its benefits. I was talking to someone yesterday about the *Carry On* movies and thinking I must go and look at those again. Whereas twenty years ago access to *Carry On Cowboy*, for example, would have been about zero, now it's very easy to get hold of.

AA: Your newest collection, *One Thousand Things Worth Knowing*, has a line: 'Source is to leak as Ireland is to debt.' Could you tell us a little more about this relationship?

PM: The reasons Ireland got into debt are complex. They have to do with the world economy: no one stands alone in that regard. But it was a very local thing, too, in that forty or fifty bankers who lent and borrowed money are largely responsible for the Irish problem. Everybody knows who they are, their names have been published. Really they haven't had to pay any price for the trouble they caused. The government was also responsible for bailing out a bank, which frankly it shouldn't have.

SG: There seems to be a greater willingness in the US to prosecute financial misdemeanours in a way that is perhaps not the case in Europe.

PM: Absolutely. In the *Financial Times* recently there was a piece about four very large banks that have just been fined for improper behaviour.

And one of them was more-or-less quoted as saying, 'If you're not doing something shady then you're not in the game.' What a terrible example to set the culture at large – the children in particular.

SG: Do you think this economic mindset has informed other areas of culture – education, for example?

PM: It would be nice to think that a government in a civilized country could provide free education and free healthcare – in that sense I would be what used to be called a 'socialist'. In the UK, where we're conducting this interview, it's quite clear that no government is interested in education. Public money is not going to be given to education, unless something quite dramatic – like the Labour Party becoming a socialist party again – should happen. I don't trust any of these governments to support education. I'm afraid that, for better or worse, the privatisation of education is going to have to happen.

SG: State funding for education is rather different in the US.

PM: There are state-funded schools and universities in the US, but many of them have developed their own funding systems. That kind of set up is going to take a while, if indeed it ever happens, to take off in this country, because people don't want to give money. But the universities will not be able to do their job properly until they can say to the government, 'Sorry, we don't need your money – take a hike.' I happen to teach for a university that's very wealthy. But it uses its money in very inspired and inspiring ways. If you get into Princeton and you can afford to pay to-wards your education, you pay, but if you can't pay anything at all, that's fine – they pay for it. They don't give you a loan [as they do in the UK], though: they give you a grant, so they are not expecting the money back. The student loan history in the UK, and to some extent in the US, and (if they don't watch themselves) in Ireland, is a really problematic thing. They can never expect people to give freely to universities when they owe them so much money: a culture of giving is not going to happen. In terms of the arts, the Arts Council is cutting things everywhere you look. People are at a loss to find other ways of funding the arts. They really need to develop new structures to get tax-free funding from donors and other institutions.

SG: In 2011 Alice Oswald withdrew her collection *Memorial* from the TS Eliot Prize because the Poetry Book Society had accepted money from a hedge fund. She was worried, I suppose, about the prevalence of unchecked private interests in funding the arts.

PM: Fair enough. But if she's worried about that she should be just as worried about unchecked public interests. Nothing is clean. Is there clean money anywhere? I don't think so. If you are worried about one's government, why not withdraw from anything to do with the UK government? Where do you draw the line? God knows where this T-shirt I'm wearing was made. Should I stop wearing it? I suppose I could.

AA: The internet has made many things easier to find, and Google is now at the critic's fingertips. Has this availability of information affected what in your poetry you might consider obscure or arcane?

PM: It's true that a number of my poems refer to things that are less well known than others, various usages of language, particularly Hiberno-English – though not only that – and elements of the wider cultural life of Ireland, and America, which are referents for me now I've lived there for a long time. I suppose this is true of each person. Each person brings with them a particular history. To the extent that one might write that out, and try to figure things out about one's life, it's almost inevitable that in each of our cases there will be some arcane references. Where are you from, for example?

AA: Near Blackpool, in the North West of England.

PM: And what was Blackpool like when you were a kid? It's not all that long ago but it must have been very different?

AA: I don't know actually, Blackpool is a funny case ...

PM: But everywhere is a funny case. What Blackpool means now is not the same as what it meant twenty years ago, and certainly not fifty years ago. So if I talk about Blackpool in a poem set fifty years ago, I'm thinking about what Blackpool meant to someone from Northern Ireland who grew up at that time, watching British TV, and with the whole history of seaside humour and music hall. So as someone from Ireland who was brought up almost as much on Gaelic culture as French culture or Latin poetry, never mind English poetry and American poetry and poetry in translation from the world over, it's inevitable that there will be a wide range of cultural reference.

It's natural for me to use a word in Gaelic if that's the appropriate word. If I use the word *meitheal* – the specific term for a group of workers who helped each other out at harvest time – one wouldn't be using the word because it seems fanciful or arcane, but because that's the word.

SG: Is the choice of word sometimes influenced by sound as much as sense?

PM: Rarely. I know it may seem that way, that the rhymes inform things – as they probably do from time to time. But when you're writing a poem there is a whole host of things in orbit, as it were: how this word follows that word, why the line ends there, what it means to me, what it might mean to someone coming down the street. Can I use *meitheal*? If I use it there is going to be a bit of a problem – most people are not going to understand that, nobody in Ireland would understand that, never mind anywhere else. In fact there was a whole range of words in Ireland for the same phenomenon; it actually varied from place to place in Ireland as to which word one used. In this era, one could actually allow the word *meitheal* into the poem with more equanimity than one would have thirty years ago, because you know that if somebody wants to find out what it means they can find out immediately. I don't have any problem with Dante or Shakespeare or Robert Frost or Elizabeth Bishop using a very particular term, or a precise term being used by a newspaper reporter. So why should I be bothered by this?

AA: Frost and Bishop are among the poets you mentioned in your Oxford lecture series, *The End of the Poem*. It strikes me that you came rather late to poetry criticism. Was it enjoyable to do?

PM: It was quite challenging. Particularly if one's not really a *bona fide* academic, as I am not. When Seamus Heaney was Professor of Poetry at Oxford, I remember running into him somewhere and asking him what his next lecture was going to be about. He said, 'Well actually, I don't know,' and I thought to myself, 'I can't do that.' So I had a plan from the outset, which I set down in the first lecture in fact, but then I ended up making the whole thing up as I went along.

Aspects of it are slightly tongue-in-cheek, and certainly are thought by some to be more than that – quite outrageous. But my view is, if you want somebody who is a conventional academic or poet-academic, there are all sorts of people you could find. I am not going to be that person. I'm going to find something interesting to do, in a non-conventional way. And if people want to come and hear it, fine, and if they don't, that's fine too. As a student I always enjoyed lectures that focussed on one poem: you could play around with it, go back and forth over it, it was always there, you had it in front of you. I've always enjoyed the high-jinks associated with that, with the adventure of reading, and the revelations one has as a reader.

AA: So it's one of the tasks of criticism, as you see it, to convey an infectious enjoyment of the text – to carry your audience with you on this 'adventure'?

PM: I like to think so. I don't necessarily think that all those poems I wrote about were the greatest poems ever written. They just happen to be poems where I thought, 'If I take this particular line, actually it might be useful or interesting to read that in a particular way.' I never really knew exactly what I was going to say about any of them. But I certainly don't dislike any of them; I like all of them. There could have been fifteen different poems. I think the lectures were usually quite admiring of the poem in hand. Anyone can dismantle anything – it's easy. You can take a Shakespeare sonnet and say, 'I'm not so sure about line five …' There's very little that can't be dismantled, or mocked.

SG: You mentioned Seamus Heaney's lectures: would they be a good example of this celebratory reading?

PM: Sure. I don't think Seamus had many public, or indeed private, pronouncements where he was down on something.

SG: They're wonderfully attentive to the poems, as well.

PM: Yes. Seamus Heaney taught me at one point, but the people who taught him also taught me in some cases. There was a bit of an age difference, of course, but we were actually brought up in the same New Critical or 'Practical Criticism' tradition. 'Line one has this image,' say, and you'd be kind of riffing on things. The big critics for us were [IA] Richards and [FR] Leavis and [William] Empson. I suppose Empson's a kind of hero of mine: on the one hand a kind of lunatic, and on the other hand you're thinking, 'Wow, that's really interesting.' I suppose on a good day I would like think that maybe somebody would say that about some of my stuff, too. I can see why they'd say it's lunatic and that's fine, it doesn't bother me. I understand that. Nobody's going to go to war over this; nobody's going to die because of some critical comment I've made. I hope.

SG: Your poetry seems very interested in mistakes, and in the cultivation of error.

PM: There's a lot of correcting. Is that what you mean?

SG: I'm thinking of lines like 'For "you" read "ewe."'

PM: Ah yes, I don't know about that really. That's a poem that harkens back, if one's feeling well disposed, to something I did a few years ago, which I usually don't do – wittingly anyway. There was a poem called 'Errata' which was made up of these corrections or errata.

AA: Is there ever an erotic dimension to these errors? I'm remembering that wonderful line in 'The Little Black Book': 'I fluttered, like an erratum slip, between her legs.'

PM: Yes. That's a ghazal, which as you know often has some sort of erotic charge. They say it has more to do with non-physical love, but I think in many of them there is an erotic charge. I'm not sure how I found myself writing that ghazal, but as it embarked on itself, I thought to myself, why not just do an erotic one and just go for broke? Forget about political correctness and what your mother's going to say. So what was your question – is there an autobiographical element to errors?

AA: No, I asked if there was an erotic element.

PM: Oh! Well I'd say there's an erotic element and perhaps an autobio-graphical element, too …

AA: For 'erotic' read 'autobiographical'?

PM: Maybe. You know, at various times along the way I've been inter-ested, as I am sure many people have, and this might be true of all poems at all times, in what happens between things – interstitially, as they say. Maybe that's where poems reside anyway – between the words. I'm sure some wag has said that any number of times.

But to build on that, there was a point in terms of autobiography and the erotic. I was involved some years ago with a woman called Mary Farl Powers, and I started writing some poems in which she featured, and then we broke up. The poems were published in a pamphlet called *The Wishbone*. There were a couple of poems in it – one called 'Bears' and another called 'The Ox', I think – that are in little sections with asterisks between them. And it's almost as though the poems are really all in the asterisks. I didn't publish them in a collection – I stopped going down that road for some reason – but maybe that's another way of talking about these misunderstandings. Between the cup and the lip, something happens.

AA: Or between the conscious and the unconscious?

PM: Oh yes.

AA: 'For "Freud" read "feud"'…

PM: Is that from the most recent collection?

AA: It is. Are you influenced by Freud in any way?

PM: Yes, probably. I've read a certain amount of Freud, and yes, he certainly is interested in that, isn't he? It seems very sane to me. I know Freud's reputation has slipped a little in certain quarters, but I think he's very interesting. His descriptions of unconscious connections and word usages and slippages that you're describing seem very plausible to me. I don't think it's a matter of opinion – this stuff happens, and I think it's revelatory. Not only does it happen but one may deduce something from it. Whether or not one would always go to the same extent that Freud takes his deductions, I doubt it really. But they are somewhat useful.

AA: Errors are 'portals of discovery', as Stephen Dedalus puts it. Is the error or the slip for you something that occasions the discovery of something else?

PM: Absolutely. There's a famous story of Joyce himself, while Beckett was working with him briefly. As Joyce was dictating something to Beckett – 'Riverrun, past Eve and Adam's', or whatever – there was a knock at the door, to which Joyce answered: 'Come in.' Beckett was reading it back that evening – 'Riverrun, past Eve and Adam's, come in …' – and Joyce says, 'Hold on, what's that "come in"?' Beckett says, 'I'm pretty sure that's what you said,' and Joyce says, 'OK, we'll keep it in.' I believe it's still in there somewhere.

AA: On a different topic, is this the first of your collections to include exclamation marks? There's one in 'We Love the Horse Because its Haunch', for example: '(Mesgegra, Oh my God!)'.

PM: I don't know, is the answer to that! No, now I think about it, I don't think it is; I think there's one in *Mules*. But Mesgegra, now, that's funny, but you've got to do a bit of work to get the comedy. Mesgegra was a Celtic warrior whose brains had been mixed with lime to form what they called a 'brain ball'. A particular warrior, Cet mac Mágach, hurled it at another hero, Conor MacNessa, and it stuck there; and they decided against removing it because it would be too dangerous. Then one day he got terrible news, and he started to shake and the thing fell out of his head and he died. The news was that the day was Good Friday, and that Christ had died.[1] So these two historical events were intertwined.

But to return to the exclamation mark. It's a bit like putting things in capital letters – it's thought to be not quite kosher. There are two sources that got me onto it, and got me thinking about how little used it was. One was Jan Morris, the travel writer, who I met in some far-flung corner of the world, and she was talking about the glories of the exclamation mark. The other great example was one of my wife's family members, Helene Hanff, who in another life had been working on what turned out to be the first production of *Oklahoma!*. The show had been running out of town under some other name [*Away We Go*] and had not done very well. They brought it to New York and decided, the day before it opened, to change the name to *Oklahoma*. And then, in the middle of the night, they decided they were going to change it once again to *Oklahoma!* with an exclamation mark. Now, that's an instance of an exclamation mark being rather brilliantly used. I don't think we can say, as one might like to, that the exclamation mark is a non-starter. Though I don't remember where the other exclamation marks are in the new collection. One doesn't usually sit around reading the poems after they're done.

SG: Though you do revisit a couple of earlier poems, most notably 'Cuba', in the new book.

PM: Yes, that's right. Well, we [Paul Muldoon and his daughter, Dorothy] went to Cuba, and I was trying to think of a title for the poem and I thought, why not?

SG: Is there something about the experience of being a father, and a father of a young adult, that informs the idea of revisiting the earlier work?

PM: I hadn't thought of that. Yes, that's right. Freud again, I suppose. You know, years ago, a friend of mine, since dead unfortunately, and indeed the subject of an elegy, said to me 'How's May?' And I said 'May?' And he said, 'May, your sister, from "Cuba"', and I said 'Oh, no, there's no such person, that's all made up!' So yes and no, is the answer to your question.

Notes
1) Muldoon refers to this story in *To Ireland, I* (Oxford University Press, 2000), p. 37.

Louis de Paor

HATAÍ

> Hold on to me and we'll both drown
> — John Berryman

ar thugais fé ndeara
gléas a gcuid gruaige,
leicne is ingní daite,
        súile lasta
ar aon dath is gearradh
leis na héadaí nua geala,
áthas ag sileadh leo
ó rinn go sáil:

na mná meánaosta
atá ar tí a leanaí
is a bhfearaibh
a fhágaint
iata suas
i mbarr an tí
mar a bhfuaireadar
pé ní a bhí uathu
ar feadh na mblian
ná raibh a fhios acu féin
cad é nó go bhfuaireadar é?

níor thug, arsa tú
go tur, ag imeacht
an doras amach
cumhracht uait
a chuirfeadh
adharc ar nóinín,
hata *vintage* anuas
ar leathshúil ghlas
a bhfuil doimhneas
na mara fós inti:

fothraigh bád
is fear, mná
ag gol gan stop,
buachaill amháin

ag dul faoi
arís is arís eile
ded bhuíochas:

ba dhóbair dó
bá ionat tráth

HATS OFF

> *Hold on to me and we'll both drown*
> — John Berryman

have you noticed
how their hair shines,
the colour of their cheeks
and nails, eyes lit,
shaped and shaded
to match their bright
new clothes, happiness
dripping from them,
head to toe

the middle-aged women
who are about to leave
their husbands & children
locked up in the attic
where they found
whatever they were looking for
all these years
only they didn't realise
what it was till they found it?

I have not, you say,
heading out the door,
smelling so sweet
you'd give a daisy
bad thoughts,
a vintage hat
tilted over one eye
that is still sea-deep

full of shipwrecks
and manwrecks
women crying
and one boy
who keeps going
down again and again
no matter how
you try to stop him:

he almost
drowned
in you once

Caitríona O'Reilly

THE DIAMOND CUTTER

He cannot calculate what it has done to him,
his knowledge of the mathematics of indifference
set going one day out of idleness or mischief.

If the universe is a struck chord
then it is deafening, abyssal. It silences all he had thought was his
when he began: what was meant by morning;

what birdsong insisted on; everything that promised
to turn and shine in shoals, of one mind;
his mother's hands. Her eyes milky as stones.

Instead, he turns his face from the world,
the whole sun-flensed ashpit of it,
towards his instruments of magnification, his loupe

through which he stares down fathoms of carbon,
down the depthless clarity of star-sinter,
a lattice of atoms so tightly packed they vanish.

He deals in invisibility, like the mystic
inferring his god from the silence of held breath,
measuring its exact, scintillant outline,

its location on his scale of brilliance.
He is obsessive about flaws, which he terms *inclusions*:
grain lines, fractures, feathers, fingerprints,

twinning wisps, clouds, knots, needles;
finding his way is to advance by subtraction,
that what is lost in weight is gained in light.

Caitríona O'Reilly

TOLKIEN IN THIEPVAL

Under the lost leaves, it seems clear
the absence of love is not nothingness
but a universe filled with noise:
the air concussive with iron and lead,
the crump of shells throwing up geysers of soil
or bursting into a thousand steel needles.
All this happens in love's withdrawal,
with a vast inrushing roar.

Does the light itself possess a shadow?
Or is it in the leaves' invisible flickering, so like ripples,
a solitary bird singing in the abyss?
Boys who, just yesterday, felt like us,
loved hotly, tasted the salt trickle of fear,
have become unreachable and strange;
the territory of death has annexed them,
expanding its borders across their pale faces
staring upwards through the waters of flooded craters.

That something of this will remain *in absentia*
I understand: as a struck bell's hollowness
or a finger drawn around the rim of an empty glass
send waves of resonance travelling towards the stars forever;
so we will hoard the white scars scrawled
across our bodies, intricate as script, until we are old men:
as a healed wood bears on its leaves the tracery of love.

Notes on Contributors

Simon Armitage has published ten collections of poetry, including *Paper Aeroplane: Selected Poems 1989-2014* (Faber and Faber, 2014), and his acclaimed translation of *Sir Gawain and the Green Knight* (Faber and Faber, 2009). He is Professor of Poetry at the University of Sheffield, and in 2015 was elected Professor of Poetry at Oxford University.

Paul Batchelor is a lecturer in English Literature and Creative Writing at Durham University. His last publication was *The Love Darg* (Clutag Press, 2014).

Amanda Bell was highly commended for the Patrick Kavanagh Poetry Award in 2015 and 2016, and selected for Poetry Ireland's 2016 Introductions Series. Her collection of haibun and haiku, *Undercurrents,* came out this year from Alba Publishing. Her illustrated book for children, *The Lost Library Book*, is forthcoming from The Onslaught Press.

Ciaran Berry's most recent collection is *The Dead Zoo*, published by The Gallery Press in 2013. Newer work has appeared recently in *Poetry*, *The Southern Review*, and *Ecotone*. He lives with his wife and sons in Hartford, Connecticut, where he teaches at Trinity College.

Rachael Boast's *Sidereal* (Picador, 2011) won the Forward Prize for Best First Collection and the Seamus Heaney Centre for Poetry Prize. *Pilgrim's Flower* (Picador, 2013) was shortlisted for the Griffin Prize. She was co-editor of *The Echoing Gallery: Bristol Poets and Art in the City* (Redcliffe Press, 2013). *Void Studies* is just published by Picador and has been shortlisted for the TS Eliot Prize.

Colette Bryce's latest collection, *The Whole & Rain-domed Universe*, received a Christopher Ewart-Biggs Award in memory of Seamus Heaney. Her *Selected Poems* will be published by Picador in 2017.

Dom Bury has been published in poetry magazines and anthologies including *Poetry Wales, Ambit, The North, Magma Poetry* and *The Best British Poetry 2014* (Salt Publishing). He won the Magma Poetry Prize in 2013. He is a 2016 Jerwood/Arvon Mentee, and the recipient of a 2016 Eric Gregory Award.

Anthony Caleshu's third collection, *The Victor Poems*, was published by Shearsman Books in 2015. He is editor of the forthcoming *In The Air: Essays On The Poetry of Peter Gizzi* (Wesleyan University Press, 2017). He lives in England where he directs the MA in Creative Writing programme and is Professor of Poetry at Plymouth University.

Gerry Cambridge's latest book of poems is *Notes for Lighting a Fire* (Happen*Stance*, 2012). *The Printed Snow*, on typesetting poetry, appeared in 2015. *The Dark Horse: The Making of a Little Magazine* (Happen*Stance*, 2016), is his anecdotal history of the poetry journal he founded in an Ayrshire caravan in 1995.

Kimberly Campanello was born in Elkhart, Indiana, and is a dual American and Irish citizen. Her books include *Imagines* (New Dublin Press), *Strange Country* (The Dreadful Press), and *Hymn to Kālī* (Eyewear). ZimZalla will publish *MOTHERBABYHOME* in 2017. She is a Lecturer in Creative Writing at York St John University.

David Clink has published four collections of poetry; the latest is *The Role of Lightning in Evolution* (Chizine Publications, 2016). He hosts and organizes the annual Dead Poets Society Night in Toronto. His poem, 'A sea monster tells his story', won the Aurora Award for Best Poem/Song in 2013.

Joey Connolly lives in London, where he manages the Poetry Book Fair. His work has appeared in *The Sunday Times*, *Poetry Review*, *Best British Poetry 2014* (Salt Publishing), and been broadcast on BBC Radio 4. He received an Eric Gregory Award in 2012, and his first collection, *Long Pass*, is forthcoming from Carcanet Press.

Louis de Paor's most recent collections are *The Brindled Cat and the Nightingale's Tongue* (Bloodaxe, 2014), and *Grá Fiar* (Coiscéim, 2016). *Leabhar na hAthghabhála: Poems of Repossession* (Bloodaxe Books, 2016), a bilingual selection of twentieth-century poetry in Irish which he edited, was a Recommended Translation of the Poetry Book Society for Summer 2016.

Moyra Donaldson, from Co Down, has published six collections of poetry including *Selected Poems* (2012) and *The Goose Tree* (2014), both from Liberties Press. Her latest project was a collaboration with photographic artist Victoria J Dean, resulting in an exhibition and the publication *Abridged 0-36 Dis-Ease.*

Miriam Gamble lectures in Creative Writing at Edinburgh University. Her collections are *The Squirrels Are Dead* (2010), which won a Somerset Maugham Award in 2011, and *Pirate Music* (2014), both published by Bloodaxe Books.

Jo Gill is Professor of Twentieth-Century and American Literature at the University of Exeter. She has written extensively on modern and contemporary poetry and, with the support of a Fellowship from the Leverhulme Trust, is completing a book on *Modern American Poetry and the Architectural Imagination.*

Richard Hayes is Head of the School of Humanities at Waterford Institute of Technology, where he also teaches English. He has published many articles on Irish and American literature, and has a particular interest in regional writing.

Paul Henry's sixth collection, *Boy Running*, was published in 2015 by Seren Books and shortlisted for Wales Book of the Year 2016. The same publisher recently reprinted *The Brittle Sea: New and Selected Poems*. His website is **www.paulhenrywales.co.uk**.

Seán Hewitt's poetry has been published in *Poetry*, *Poetry Review* and the *New Statesman*, amongst other outlets. He is a Ph.D. candidate at the Institute of Irish Studies, University of Liverpool. He won a Northern Writers Award in 2016.

Matt Howard lives in Norwich, where he works for the Royal Society for the Protection of Birds. Matt is also a steering group member of New Networks for Nature, an eco-organisation that asserts the central importance of landscape and nature in our cultural life. His debut pamphlet, *The Organ Box*, was published by Eyewear Publishing in 2014.

Evan Jones, a Canadian poet, has lived in Manchester since 2005. His most recent collection is *Paralogues* (Carcanet Press, 2012).

Luke Kennard is the author of five collections of poetry; the latest is *Cain* (Penned in the Margins, 2016). His first novel will be published by 4th Estate in March 2017. He lectures at the University of Birmingham.

Simon Kew has been published in *Iota, The Rialto, Agenda* and *Magma Poetry*.

Igor Klikovac is a Bosnian poet living in London since 1993. His work is published in Bosnia, countries of former Yugoslavia, Britain, and elsewhere. His poetry is included in a number of anthologies, including *The Souls of the Dead are Taking the Best Seats* (Luath Press, 2004); and *Scar on the Stone: Contemporary Poetry from Bosnia* (Bloodaxe Books, 1998), edited by Chris Agee.

Alice Lyons is a poet and visual artist whose work has been published in books, as public art projects, films, and gallery installations. Recipient of the Patrick Kavanagh Award, the Ireland Chair of Poetry Bursary and an IFTA nomination in animation, she is currently Fellow in Poetry and New Media at Harvard University's Radcliffe Institute for Advanced Study. Her most recent collection is *The Breadbasket of Europe* (Veer Books, 2016). She is also curator of the Poetry Now festival.

John McAuliffe's fourth book *The Way In* (The Gallery Press) was joint winner of the Michael Hartnett Award 2016. He is working with Igor Klikovac on the translation of Klikovac's third book of poetry, *Stockholm Syndrome*.

John McDonald, living in Edinburgh, is a retired stonemason from Aberdeen who is internationally known in the haiku world. His latest book, in association with IMRAM, is *Tea wi the Abbot*, haiku in Scots with transcreations in Irish by Gabriel Rosenstock (The Onslaught Press, 2016).

Medbh McGuckian recently retired from lectureship at the Seamus Heaney Centre for poetry, Queen's University, Belfast. Her collection *Blaris Moor* (The Gallery Press, 2015) was shortlisted for the *Irish Times* Poetry Now Award. *The Unfixed Horizon: New Selected Poems* was published in 2015 by Wake Forest University Press.

John McKernan lives in West Virginia and Florida. His most recent book is a Selected poems, *Resurrection of the Dust* (The Backwaters Press, 2007). He has published poems in *The Atlantic, The Paris Review, The New Yorker, Virginia Quarterly Review, The Hudson Review*, and many other magazines.

Mary Montague has two poetry collections, *Black Wolf on a White Plain* (Summer Palace Press, 2001) and *Tribe* (Dedalus Press, 2008). She completed a Ph.D. on birdsong in 2014. She lives in Belfast and is working on her third poetry collection and on a novel.

Sinéad Morrissey is the author of five collections of poetry, the most recent of which (*Parallax*, from Carcanet Press, 2013) was awarded the TS Eliot and the *Irish Times* Poetry Prizes. *Parallax and Selected Poems* was published by Farrar, Straus and Giroux in 2015, and was a finalist in the 2016 National Book Critics Circle Award.

Paul Muldoon, born in Co Armagh, now lives in New York. A former radio and television producer for the BBC in Belfast, he has taught at Princeton University for almost thirty years. He is the author of twelve collections of poetry, including *Moy Sand and Gravel* (Faber and Faber, 2002), for which he won the 2003 Pulitzer Prize. His most recent book is *Selected Poems 1968-2014* (Faber and Faber, 2016).

John Murphy's first collection, *The Book Of Water*, was published by Salmon Poetry in 2012. His second collection is *The Language Hospital* (Salmon Poetry, 2016).

Doireann Ní Ghríofa is a bilingual writer working in Irish and English. Among her awards are the Rooney Prize for Irish Literature, the Michael Hartnett Prize, and the Ireland Chair of Poetry bursary. Her collection *Oighear* is forthcoming from Coiscéim in 2017.

Kate Noakes's sixth collection, *Paris as Stage*, is forthcoming from Eyewear Publishing in 2017. She is an elected member of the Welsh Academy and her website (**www.boomslangpoetry.blogspot.com**) is archived by the National Library of Wales. She lives and writes in London and Paris.

Jean O'Brien's fifth collection, *Fish on a Bicycle: New and Selected Poems*, is just published by Salmon Poetry. Her work has appeared in many journals and anthologies, and she has received many awards. She read for an M.Phil. in Trinity College, Dublin, and tutors in creative writing.

Sean O'Brien's eighth collection of poems is *The Beautiful Librarians* (Bloodaxe Books, 2015). It was a PBS Choice, joint winner of the Roehampton Poetry Prize, and shortlisted for the TS Eliot Prize. He is Professor of Creative Writing at Newcastle University. The poem printed in this edition of *Poetry Ireland Review* is part of *Hammersmith*, a book-length poem to be published by Picador.

Mary O'Donnell is a poet and fiction-writer. Her seventh collection, *Those April Fevers* (2015), was published by Arc Publications. She was a co-winner of the Irodalmi Jelen Award for Poetry in Translation (Hungary) in 2012. She currently teaches Poetry at NUI Galway's MA in Creative Writing, and is a member of Aosdána (**www.maryodonnell.com**).

Bernard O'Donoghue was born in Co Cork. Since 1965 he has lived in Oxford where he taught medieval literature and modern Irish poetry. The most recent of his seven volumes of poems is *The Seasons of Cullen Church*, published by Faber and Faber in 2016.

Lani O'Hanlon is a dancer and the author of *Dancing the Rainbow* (Mercier Press, 2007). She has an MA from Lancaster University, with poetry published in the journals *Southword*, *The Stinging Fly*, *The Moth*, *Skylight 47*, *Mslexia*, and *Poetry*, and the anthologies *Small Lives* (Poddle Publications, 2014) and *Hallelujah for 50ft Women* (Bloodaxe Books, 2015). She has also read on RTÉ's *Sunday Miscellany* programme.

Caitríona O'Reilly is originally from Wicklow and now lives in Lincoln. She has worked as a teacher of literature and as an editor and critic. She has published three collections of poetry, *The Nowhere Birds* (Bloodaxe Books, 2001); *The Sea Cabinet* (Bloodaxe Books, 2006); and most recently *Geis* (Bloodaxe Books, 2015) which was shortlisted for the 2016 Pigott Prize, and won the *Irish Times* Poetry Now Award in 2016.

Jacob Polley has published four books of poems with Picador, most recently *Jackself* (2016), and a novel, *Talk of the Town* (Pan Macmillan, 2009). Born in Cumbria, he now lives in Newcastle and teaches at Newcastle University.

Michael Symmons Roberts was born in 1963 in Preston, Lancashire. His poetry has won the Forward Prize, the Costa Poetry Prize and the Whitbread Poetry Award, and been shortlisted for the Griffin International Poetry Prize and the TS Eliot Prize. He is a Fellow of the Royal Society of Literature, and of the English Association. He has published two novels, and is Professor of Poetry at Manchester Metropolitan University.

David Romanda lives in Kawasaki City, Japan. His work has appeared in *Ambit*, *The Moth*, and *PN Review*.

Gabriel Rosenstock is a poet, tankaist and haikuist. His latest book *Judgement Day* (The Onslaught Press) consists of ekphrastic haiku in Irish and English in response to the controversial collages of Karl Waldmann.

Peter Sirr lives in Dublin where he works as a freelance writer and teaches a course in literary translation for the Translation Centre in Trinity College, Dublin. His most recent collections of poems are *Sway: Versions of Poems from the Troubadour Tradition* (The Gallery Press, 2016), and *The Rooms* (The Gallery Press, 2014), shortlisted for the *Irish Times* Poetry Now Award and the Pigott Poetry Prize. He is a member of Aosdána.

Gerard Smyth's recent collections from Dedalus Press include *A Song of Elsewhere* (2015) and *The Fullness of Time: New and Selected Poems* (2010). *After Easter*, a sequence of poems in response to 1916 with a drawing by artist Brian Maguire, was recently published by The Salvage Press, and *The Yellow River*, a collection of poems set in Co Meath accompanied by watercolours by artist Seán McSweeney, is due to be published by the Solstice Arts Centre, Navan, in 2017. He is a member of Aosdána and Poetry Editor of *The Irish Times*.

Fiona Sze-Lorrain is the author of three books of poetry, most recently *The Ruined Elegance* (Princeton University Press, 2016), a finalist for the *Los Angeles Times* Book Prize. Her translation of Yi Lu's *Sea Summit* (Milkweed, 2016), is shortlisted for the Best Translated Book Award. A zheng harpist, she lives in France.

Jacqueline Thompson recently completed a Ph.D. in Creative Writing at the University of Edinburgh. Her poems have appeared in publications including *The Scotsman*, *New Writing Scotland*, *Gutter*, *Double Bill* (Red Squirrel Press, 2014) and *From Arthur's Seat* (Egg Box Publishing, 2016). She is currently on the shortlist for the Melita Hume Prize.

Zoë Brigley Thompson is from Wales, but is currently visiting assistant professor at the Ohio State University. She has two poetry collections from Bloodaxe Books, *The Secret* (2007) and *Conquest* (2012), both Poetry Book Society Recommendations.

Rebecca Watts was born in Suffolk in 1983 and currently lives in Cambridge. Her debut collection, *The Met Office Advises Caution*, was published by Carcanet Press in 2016, and is a Poetry Book Society Recommendation.

Joseph Woods has published three award-winning books of poetry and a fourth is forthcoming. A former director of Poetry Ireland, he lives in Harare, Zimbabwe with his family.